D0497957

The Probable and the Marvelous

The Probable
and the Marvelous

*Blake, Wordsworth, and the
Eighteenth-Century Critical Tradition*

Wallace Jackson

The University of Georgia Press
Athens

The University of Georgia Press, Athens 30602

Set in 11 on 13 point Mergenthaler Bembo type
Printed in the United States of America

Library of Congress Cataloging in Publication Data

Jackson, Wallace, 1930–
   The probable and the marvelous.
   Bibliography.
   Includes index.
   1. English poetry—18th century—History and
criticism. 2. Criticism—Great Britain—History. 3.
Blake, William, 1757–1827—Criticism and interpretation. 4. Wordsworth, William, 1770–1850—Criticism and interpretation. I. Title.

PR571.J3   821'.6'09   77-17807
          ISBN 0-8203-0439-5

Parts of chapters four and five are reprinted from
"Wordsworth and His Predecessors: Private Sensations
and Public Tones," *Criticism* 17 (1975): 41–58, by
permission of the Wayne State University Press; and
from "William Blake in 1789: Unorganized *Innocence*,"
Modern Language Quarterly 33 (1972): 396–404, by
permission of the editor.

Contents

Acknowledgments

I would like first to thank the English Department of Duke University for granting me release time from my teaching duties to complete the book. I am also obliged to the Duke University Research Council for its willingness to find readers outside the university for my study. To Professors Leigh DeNeef, Oliver Ferguson, Gerald Monsman, and Clyde Ryals, I am very grateful for their careful and attentive reading of the text; many of their numerous suggestions they will find incorporated in my work. I have a long-standing debt to Professor Arthur Scouten of the University of Pennsylvania for his patient encouragement and good friendship. Karen Orchard of the University of Georgia Press has been extremely considerate and helpful in seeing this study through the various stages leading to publication. Most of all I wish to thank Myrna Jackson, whose critical acumen has time and again searched the limitations of this argument. Without her scrutiny this book, whatever its shortcomings, would be yet less than it is.

1
Introduction

Modern scholarship and criticism have found middle and later eighteenth-century poetry uniquely limited and only occasionally first-rate. Among the very best poems are Thomas Gray's "Elegy Written in a Country Churchyard," William Collins's "Ode on the Poetical Character," perhaps Samuel Johnson's "Vanity of Human Wishes," and, charitably, Christopher Smart's complexly designed "A Song to David." Of competent performances there are many, but of major poems or poets there are few. It is an age in which, for one reason or another, the productions of the most promising poets were often limited in number and quality. Gray's poems are few, his letters many; early in his life Collins declined into madness; Joseph and Thomas Warton never surpassed, perhaps never equaled, their juvenile poetry. William Cowper's religious melancholy vitiated his energies and directed him, subjectless, to his longest and most sustained work. Of such literary oddities as James Macpherson and Thomas Chatterton twentieth-century criticism has had little to say, for the very good reason that there is little to say.

It is no wonder that the years between the death of Pope in 1744 and the emergence of Blake and Wordsworth in the last decade of the century have seemed to most students a time of relative poetic decline. It is equally unsurprising that the period has sponsored highly divergent and inconsistent appraisal. Alternately it has been called preromantic, post-Augustan, and, most recently, an age of sensibility. We are told that it weakly precedes greatness or feebly descends from it. Northrop Frye, taking a somewhat different tack, argues for the inherent poetic coherence of the age and for the greatness of its products.[1] Such views constitute the spectrum of present opinion, but they may be further amplified.

Stuart Chase, for example, begins with the not uncommon notion that in some sense or senses the poetry of the later eighteenth century failed to provide "an adequately complicated mythology," and that the cost was reflected in "the tremendous and destructive intellectual upheavals at the end of the eighteenth century." Louis Bredvold has a somewhat different idea of failure in mind when, addressing himself to the cult of sensibility, to the man of feeling in the later years of the period, he remarks on the emergence of "all those spiritual diseases which come under the category of *mal du siècle*." Bertrand Bronson, however, offers the view that nothing was really wrong at all, that if we did not know that Romanticism followed upon the end of the eighteenth century "should we not quite naturally be seeing the eighteenth century in quite another than the customary view: as in fact a period when the spirit of Classicism steadily *refined* its values, grew increasingly *assured* in its declaration of them, and never knew better their true and vital meaning and importance than when on the verge of losing them?" Just when the writers of the late eighteenth century were growing ripe and rich in the possession of their values along came Romanticism and an untimely end.[2]

Other judgments have been equally possible. Samuel Monk holds that the "difference between pre-romanticism and the romantic is largely a matter of subtlety, the measure of which can be taken by contrasting the terrors of the gothic novel and of *Christabel,* or the enthusiasm of the Blue Stockings for mountain scenery and Wordsworth's treatment of the same theme."[3] For Monk, Romanticism is a refinement upon the crudities of armchair thrills and Alpine vistas, thus something akin to a more complex emotionalism, a heightening that is more satisfactory because it is more sophisticated.

It is possible to summon these reflections as the measure of our own uneasiness with a historical period for which we have no generally satisfactory name. The purpose of this study, therefore, is to propose yet another approach to the complicated subject of English poetry and criticism in the later years of the eighteenth century, my inquiry guided by sustained reference to the informing theme of the probable and marvelous. Between the years 1750 and 1800 two revolutions in English poetry not at all irrelevant to each other occurred. The first, with which I associate chiefly the poets Collins, Gray, and the brothers Joseph and Thomas Warton, was largely encouraged and supported by a body of literary criticism that began to appear at mid-century. For both the poets and the critics, the touchstone of their movement was a decidedly more radical interest in the poetic marvelous than had been tolerated by the literary Augustans. The poets of mid-century, and the critics who encouraged them, sought an enlargement of poetic license to delineate the unbodied realities of the human spirit that the eighteenth century called the passions. In Collins, Gray, and the Wartons, the principal actors of their poetry were the furies and beneficent deities of the human mind; and by embodying them in the pageants and processions of their poetry they offered an image of human nature, which, according to their views, had departed from English poetry with Spenser, Shakespeare, and Milton.

To the Wartons, Richard Hurd, Robert Lowth, Hugh Blair, and others who shared their assumptions, something of incalculable value had vanished from English poetry. Thomas Warton's *History of English Poetry* surveyed the fine fabling and those enchantments of the imagination that had been effaced with the coming of the Restoration. Joseph War-

ton's *Essay on the Genius and Writings of Pope* argued the in-
adequacies of Augustan poetry and the Augustan ideal. Pope
was the best poet the previous age could show, and yet he was
only, Warton was to decide, a poet of the second rank. Dryden was no better. Both the *History* and the *Essay* were sound
scholarly and critical works, but at heart they were also
polemical exercises of no small importance. They set a standard for poetry; they offered the age a perspective from
which to judge a new poetry and established the values with
which the Wartons expected poetry to be informed. To a new
literature the Wartons brought the aspirations of an old, and
nothing was more basic to their purposes than to restore
English poetry to its central traditions.

Thus they resumed what they believed to be the true impulses of the native tradition in poetry, a tradition largely
distorted by their Restoration and Augustan predecessors.
By so doing, they offered both a more comprehensive appeal
to, and representation of, the diversities of human sensibility
than had been practiced by the poets, with the exception of
Milton, of the preceding hundred years. They wished to
create in poetry not a myth of human nature—for they were
not mythmakers—but an anatomy of the passions that
would reveal the magnitude of the human spirit. In this en-
deavor they were aided and abetted by such contemporary
fashions as the traditions of *ut pictura poesis,* by the sublime,
and by the growing interest in cultural and aesthetic
primitivism.

Basically the tradition of *ut pictura poesis* developed in English poetry from the demand for an immediately affective
art, and fundamentally the lyric was the literary form most
able to meet this requirement. The sublime served somewhat
similar purposes; its effect was taken to be an immediate
exaltation of spirit, an enlargement of the imagination, in its
more extreme form an aesthetic of transcendence. The grow-

ing awareness of diverse cultures reminded mid-century critics of the variations of human society; hence the need for a more capaciously appealing poetry consistent with a widening recognition of various national poetries.

More than anything else, however, the full-scale reaction to the conception of human nature—carefully established by the greatest of the Augustan humanists, Dryden, Swift, and Pope—was predicated on the conviction that to display the passions within the theater of the mind was the proper, if not the only, subject of poetry. Thus, Fear and Vengeance, Contemplation and Melancholy, Ambition and Grandeur, and other such personifications are the chief actors within the lyric dramas of mid-century. Such representations arise in response to the need to body forth those emotions and impulses determinative of human nature and human life; and they are offered by the poets as the agents of human necessity, as the variegated qualities, elemental and resident within man, that make his life what it is. These poets did not write epic or tragedy, but they characteristically set forth, and at large, the entire host of unsubstantial realities existent within the imagination. They wanted, in sum, a newly marvelous subject not divorced from probability but founded on the probabilities of human nature and justified by the evidence of past literatures.

Paradoxically, however, while they searched for the wonders within the mind, they created no myth of human identity to which such wonders could be referred. To speak metaphorically, they created a stage on which to present their actors but no action in which they could participate. Macpherson, responding somewhat differently, refurbished the remnants of Celtic epic, while Chatterton reimagined a heroic medievalism. Their activities suggest the incapacity to create a poetry of direct and immediate contemporary reference, to find an action suitable to the marvelous within the mind. And because this was so, as I will argue later at length, another revolution in poetry occurred in the closing years of the century.

This second revolution was created by Blake and Wordsworth within the framework of lyric poetry. It was built upon the foundation of Milton's major epic and involved the reimagining of the Miltonic theme, innocence and experience. Using this theme both Blake and Wordsworth refashioned the poetic marvelous to construct a myth of human nature, a myth of innocence, fall, and redemption that informs their early lyrics and Blake's *epyllia*. Both poets began again in the last decade of the century with the commonplace and familiar, reinvesting their lyrics with the narrative of everyman's journey, the passage from innocence to experience. In doing so they renewed the Miltonic vision in a manner much beyond the scope of the melancholic and musing mind of mid-century. They redefined the marvelous within the probable and suggested the sublimity of the ordinary aspects of human experience. It is fitting therefore to view both new poets within the contours of eighteenth-century literary history, for the urgencies that summoned them cannot be estimated without reference to the renaissance of mid-century.

One of the most compelling problems of Restoration and eighteenth-century criticism involved the satisfactory relation of the marvelous to the probable. Though the problem antedated seventeenth-century criticism, it became intensified by the requirements of a chastened credulity so characteristic of Restoration and Augustan criticism. It is therefore with a reconsideration of this criticism we must begin, in the expectation that it offers those materials from which a new perspective can be fashioned. To commence with the literary criticism of the later seventeenth century is to conclude—not in the least arbitrarily—with Blake and Wordsworth. It is certainly no distortion of literary history to view those great and early Romantic poets within the context of an extended debate bearing upon the theme of the probable and marvelous. Indeed, such a perception is vital and necessary for recognizing the character of the poetic revolution they initiated. More than any other single theme, the permissible limits of the marvelous consistent with the delineation of probable human action and response shaped the revaluations of mid-century and informed the purposes of the major poets of the period. It is this theme also, and the revitalized employment of it, that directed the mythopoeic lyrics of those later revolutionary poets we know as the first Romantics.

One cautionary observation may well be offered. If I could suppose an ideal reader for this study he would be well versed in Paul Fussell's *The Rhetorical World of Augustan Humanism*. My own work is no challenge to Fussell's elegant and informed commentary but a rendering of the poetic and critical history of the later eighteenth century coexistent with the surviving classical or humanist tradition. In Johnson's *Lives of the English Poets*, in Gibbon's *Roman Empire*, in Cowper's *Iliad* and *Odyssey*, in Burke's *Letter to a Noble Lord*, in Reynolds's *Discourses*, the classical tradition survives. Yet, while such works suggest no furtive existence, the humanist tradition in English letters moves perceptibly to the periphery of literature. In poetry and criticism—the specific subjects I address here—a new center has been occupied and informed by the vitality of the Wartons, Blair, Hurd, and Lowth. The reflection of their arguments and reassessments in Collins, Gray, and Macpherson defines the nearest approximation to a literary school that the middle and later years of the eighteenth century afford.

Though my subject is limited to a particular line of historical inquiry, its implications extend throughout the whole of later eighteenth-century literature. Ian Watt, speaking of

Tristram Shandy, remarks: "Faced by the apparent failure of man to live up to his alleged nature as a rational animal, and forced to be dubious about the probability of success in Locke's effort to tidy matters up, this movement ["whose greatest philosophical representative is David Hume"] turned its attention to the complexities of actual human behavior and to the mysteries of psychological identification between individuals." In another context, J. B. Beer speaks of what he calls the "other side of the eighteenth-century mind—the Gothic love of horrible sublimity and powerful destruction—for which the unregenerate Reason can find no place."[4]

Clearly, new forces were gathering in the later eighteenth century, but the recognition of them, and of their relation to Romanticism, has always been a matter of emphasis and, I might add, of critical tact. While it is unusual today to find a critic speaking of pre-Romanticism, it is quite common to find any number of scholars suggesting strange new gatherings of poetic and literary energies in the later eighteenth century. For the sake of clarity alone one wishes to avoid terminological disputes, and I have tried to circumvent such doubtful terms as post-Augustan, pre-Romantic, or sensibility to characterize the period with which I am mainly concerned. Yet in this period the dominant creative energies have been transferred from that always lightly fortified bastion we know as English Augustanism; and if such energies slowly coalesce into the untidy form or forms of Romanticism they yet retain something of what they were. All this I acknowledge while holding to my central proposition: the theme of the probable and the marvelous is not a historian's invention but a discovery. It shapes the protracted and central movement of poetry and criticism in the middle and later years; as a subject it is given substantial attention by Restoration critics and so forms an important backdrop to mid-century; and it strongly directs the character of English Romanticism in the formative stages.

Skeptical readers of this work may assume that in chapters four and five Blake and Wordsworth enter as heroes waiting in the wings. To such I would remark that I am not writing from a parti pris position. On the contrary, my treatment of these new poets is intended to suggest the terms of historical continuity in the broadest and most lucid outlines that are available to me. New poets speak to their elders, learn from them and deny them, and work with the problems that are their inheritance. Such remarks define the spirit of my engagement; the evidence that shapes these convictions is in the pages that follow.

2
The Critical Situation

There has probably been no greater demand upon poetry than that it reconcile seemingly incompatible values. It is expected to engage our emotions, yet not to offend rationality; to appeal to our appetite for the ideal and marvelous, yet not to violate probability. The prescription is as old as literary criticism; it has traditionally informed conceptions of genre and guided the development of rules governing poetic license and poetic liberty. It is deeply involved with the twofold function of the poet to please and to educate. At no time, however, was the relation between the probable and the marvelous a more lively and consistent topic of literary criticism than in the later years of the seventeenth century. The subject appeared in almost every important critical essay and no writer was wholly inattentive to it. In the criticism of the time the relation between the probable and the marvelous was joined to a historical awareness that haunts the neoclassical writer, from which he was never free, so that he moved cautiously within the liberties he claimed, keeping always one eye on the practice of those distant Greek and Roman progenitors with whom he allied himself.

The relation between the probable and the marvelous informed topics central to neoclassical criticism, topics that defined the principal articles of belief to which many later seventeenth-century writers subscribed. These are reducible to the several heads that follow.

(1) Poetry is the product of fancy and judgment working collaboratively and together constituting wit or imagination.

The dominant view of the imagination in Restoration England is the one expressed by Hobbes in his "Answer to Davenant": "Judgment begets the strength and structure and Fancy begets the ornaments of a Poem." Fancy is associated with poetic embellishment, with metaphor and boldly figurative language, but also identified as the perceptive activity in which the relation between things unlike is discovered. Invariably, fancy is linked with extravagance, and so requires the disciplining governance of the judgment; the gravity of this latter faculty reduces the tendency toward arbitrariness and improbability characteristic of the fancy. Fancy is nevertheless the source of poetic sublimity, and, as Hobbes remarked, "In a good Poem . . . the Fancy must be more eminent; because they please for the Extravagancy." The idea of fancy as a rude and somewhat wild worker is sustained in Shadwell's observation that "Fancy rough-draws, but judgement smoothes and finishes." Spenser offered the eminent example of an English poet unhappily possessed by fancy. Richard Blackmore noticed that "*Ariosto* and *Spencer,* however *great wits,* not observing this judicious Conduct of *Virgil,* nor attending to any sober Rules, are hurried with a *boundless, impetuous* Fancy over Hill and Dale, till they are both lost in a Wood of Allegories,—Allegories so *wild, unnatural,* and *extravagant,* as greatly displease the Reader."[1]

(2) The relation between fancy and judgment is joined also to the conception of the poet's mimetic function, the extent to which he must observe nature and the license he has to deviate from it. Normally this discussion was conducted in relation to epic and tragedy, and commonly romance was introduced to signify unacceptable deviations from nature. Hobbes stated the conundrum neatly: "Beyond the actual works of nature a Poet may now go; but beyond the conceived possibility of nature, never." In the Preface to *Valentinian,* Robert Wolseley attempted a definition of the central

term: "By *Nature* I do not only mean all sorts of material Objects and every species of Substance whatsoever, but also general Notions and abstracted Truths, such as exist only in the Minds of men and in the property and relation of things one to another,—in short, whatever has a Being of any kind." The definition leads, however, to another pair of terms: "*true* this expression of Nature must be that it may gain our Reason, and *lively* that it may affect our passions." Liveliness permitted excursions from a strict observance of nature, encouraged tolerance for the marvelous found in Homer and Virgil, but was insufficient to plead for those greater deviations from nature evident in Ariosto, Tasso, and Spenser. William Davenant noticed Tasso's "errors"; Hobbes objected to "impenetrable Armors, Inchanted Castles, invulnerable bodies, Iron Men, flying Horses, and a thousand other things"; and Temple dismissed impatiently "all the visionary Tribe of *Faries, Elves,* and *Goblins,* of *Sprites,* and of *Bul-beggars,* that serve only to fright Children into whatever their Nurses please."[2]

(3) Such concerns inevitably focus on the poet's obligation to speak truth. Cowley bluntly remarked that there "is not so great a *Lye* to be found in any *Poet* as the vulgar conceit of men that *Lying* is *Essential* to good *Poetry.*" More temperately, other critics distinguished between the different obligations of poet and historian. Davenant argued that "Truth narrative and past is the Idol of Historians, who worship a dead thing, and truth operative, and by effects continually alive, is the Mistris of Poets, who hath not her existence in matter but in reason." If a consensus is anywhere to be located, it is evident in Edward Phillips's reflection that the poet's duty "is to deliver feign'd things as like to truth as may be, that is to say, not too much exceeding apprehension or the belief of what is possible or likely, or positively contradictory to the truth of History."[3]

These topics define the wide-ranging criteria sponsored by

the requirement that poetry be both probable and marvelous. Representations are to be just, yet lively; the fable is to be marvelous, yet plausible (and thereby instructive); nature is to be observed, yet surpassed; the passions moved, but reason gratified. Such formulations suggest a complex poetic of tension and balance, of opposed values brought into equilibrium and not reducible beyond the terms in which they exist. They were the product of a complex revaluation of the English and classic traditions carried on by a body of writers increasingly sensing, and seeking to formulate, their own historical uniqueness. In the Restoration, Dryden was central to this activity, but he was not alone. The "more polite" age of Charles II produced a criticism that sought to align contemporary poetry, especially tragedy and epic, with the great models of classical antiquity, while at the same time it investigated the imitative possibilities in the ruder English poets of the more immediate past. In the view of these critics, Spenser was normally far less acceptable than Shakespeare. He was the victim of bad models, and Rymer's position, though excessive as usual, is not uncharacteristic: Spenser "suffer'd himself to be misled by *Ariosto;* with whom blindly rambling on *marvellous* Adventures, he makes no Conscience of *Probability.*"[4] The opinion was commonly echoed in late seventeenth-century criticism, if only because the improbabilities to be found in Spenser's romance represented an excess of the marvelous, a failure of restraint and thus of decorum, lapses by which Restoration writers recognized and stigmatized the wild and fabulous. It is therefore not surprising that when John Hughes wrote his *Essay on Allegorical Poetry* (1715), he found it useful to collect the favorable opinions of Spenser from among seventeenth-century authors, especially those held by Cowley, Milton, and Dryden.

Shakespeare represented something less of a problem for neoclassicists because his violations of probability are less frequent than Spenser's, because tragedy is inherently less improbable than romance. Rymer's reactions to Shakespeare are too well known to be rehearsed in detail, but his notorious objection to *Othello* focused upon the play as "fraught . . . with improbabilities." As early as 1672 Dryden had defined *The Winter's Tale, Love's Labours Lost,* and *Measure for Measure* as "grounded on impossibilities." Milton's epic raised some similar difficulties. Addison found much of *Paradise Lost* "temper'd with a due measure of Probability," but made "an Exception to the *Lymbo of Vanity,* with his Episode of *Sin* and *Death,* and some of the imaginary persons in his *Chaos.* These Passages are astonishing, but not credible." Much later Johnson attributed his dislike for "Lycidas" to "its inherent improbability [which] always forces dissatisfaction on the mind."[5]

Such evaluations were largely consistent with English Augustan criticism; they were the product of literary values that remained generally intact and without serious challenge until after Pope's death in 1744. But in the middle years of the century there emerged a criticism intentionally and radically disruptive of the complex equilibrium maintained by the major late seventeenth- and early eighteenth-century writers. Between the years 1753 and 1766, to date with as much historical nicety as is possible, five scholars produced work of substantial revisionist importance. Their writings constitute what might almost be called a movement of academic criticism. Thomas Warton the younger and Robert Lowth were, at different times, professors of poetry at Oxford; Joseph Warton was headmaster of Winchester College; Hugh Blair was professor of rhetoric at Edinburgh; Richard Hurd was bishop of Worcester.

Within fourteen years Thomas Warton published his *Observations on the Faerie Queene* (1754), and Joseph Warton the first volume of his influential *Essay on the Genius and Writings of Pope* (the first volume appeared anonymously in 1756; the second volume in 1782). Hugh Blair produced the *Critical Dissertation on the Poems of Ossian* (1763), and although the more impressive and voluminous work *Lectures on Rhetoric and Belles Lettres* was not published until 1783, it had been familiar matter to students at Edinburgh for the preceding twenty-four years. During this time Richard Hurd wrote the *Letters on Chivalry and Romance* (1762) and the *Dissertation on the Idea of Universal Poetry* (1766). Finally, Robert Lowth published in Latin his *Lectures on the Sacred Poetry of the Hebrews* (1753).

Such works, as the titles alone suggest, represented various literary interests and were directed to widely disparate subjects. Yet their authors shared certain common values and critical assumptions that permit us to think and speak of them as a group. The presuppositions of their criticism are fairly consistent and may be indicated as follows.

(1) Fancy is raised up to be the conspicuously eminent and dominant quality of poetry; moreover, fancy is dissociated from the restraint of judgment and allowed a liberty not previously accorded it. Spenser, as Thomas Warton observed, exemplifies the writer whose "poetry is the careless exuberance of a warm imagination and a strong sensibility." It was Spenser's "business to engage the fancy, and to interest the attention by bold and striking images," images that naturally adorn a poetry in which the "various and the marvellous were the chief sources of delight." Enthusiasm for the marvelous suggests a conception of poetry as fiction: "fiction," said Hurd, is "its soul." Its purpose is "not to delineate truth simply, but to present it in the most taking forms; not to reflect the real face of things, but to illustrate and adorn it; not to represent the fairest objects only, but to represent them in the fairest lights, and to heighten all their beauties up to the possibility of their natures; nay, to outstrip nature, and to address itself to our wildest fancy, rather than to our judg-

ment and cooler sense." Thus the "trite maxim of *following Nature* is further mistaken in applying it indiscriminately to all sorts of poetry." Poetry must appeal to the imagination, Joseph Warton remarked, through "lively pictures," the reader "whirled away by a torrent of rapid imagery." For Warton the sublime and pathetic are the "two chief nerves of all genuine poesy." To Blair the "two great characteristics of Ossian's poetry are, tenderness and sublimity," whereas Lowth discovered that the prophetic poetry of the Hebrews "rises to an uncommon pitch of sublimity," and Hurd, comparing the old romances with the Greek epics, remarked on the superior "pathos" of the former.[6]

(2) In the English tradition the great exemplars of sublime and pathetic poetry, of exuberant fancy, are Spenser, Shakespeare, and Milton. To Thomas Warton, Spenser "particularly excells in painting affright, confusion, and astonishment." To Richard Hurd, Spenser and Milton are the "two greatest of our Poets," but Spenser "still ranks highest among the Poets." Joseph Warton referred to Spenser as the "sweet and amiable allegorical poet," whose characteristics are "tender and pathetic feeling" and "a certain pleasing melancholy in his sentiments." The association among these three poets was made also to depend upon their employment of the "marvellous" and upon "Gothic manners." Even Shakespeare, said Hurd, "is greater when he uses Gothic manners and machinery, than when he employs classical: which brings us again to the same point, that the former have, by their nature and genius, the advantage of the latter in producing the *sublime*." The marvelous was further linked by Joseph Warton with "fine fabling," and the Italians cited as those to whom, "among the moderns," Englishmen owed their "true taste in poetry." Moreover, Warton wrote, "*Spenser* and *Milton* imitated the Italians, and not the French," and Spenser was "the master of Milton."[7]

(3) The invoking of Spenser, Shakespeare, and Milton was

made to serve the interests of a visionary and allegorical poetry. Thomas Warton observed: "If we take a retrospect of English poetry from the age of Spenser, we shall find, that it principally consisted in visions and allegories. Fancy was a greater friend to the dark ages, as they are called, than is commonly supposed." He cited Bishop Percy to the effect that "'our old romances of chivalry may be derived in a Lineal Descent from the ancient historical songs of the Gothic bards and scalds.'" Though Spenser derived his marvelous machineries from Ariosto and Tasso, the Italians were anticipated in their romances by the Gothic scalds. Almost inevitably this conception of the tradition and growth of fine fabling incorporated an idea of cultural primitivism, of the naturally noble feelings that such fine fabling promoted and encouraged. Warton remarked also on the Scandinavians and their "strange spirit of fantastic heroism; which however unmeaning and ridiculous it may seem, had the most serious and salutary consequence in assisting the general growth of refinement in Europe, in inculcating the principles of honor, and in teaching modes of decorum." For the purposes of polishing the manners of a nation "the powers of imagination must be awakened and exerted, to teach elegant feelings, and to heighten our natural sensibilities."[8]

(4) It followed therefore that epic and romance were genres of equal importance sharing similar purposes, the latter thus participating in the general esteem of the former: "For what are Homer's Laestrigons, and Cyclops, but bands of lawless savages, with, each of them, a Giant of enormous size at their head? And what are the Grecian Bacchus, Hercules, and Theseus but Knights-errant, the exact counter-parts of Sir Launcelot and Amadis de Gaule?" This comparison by Hurd was followed also by Joseph Warton: "To say that Amadis and Sir Tristan have a classical foundation, may at first sight appear paradoxical; but if the subject

were examined to the bottom, I am inclined to think, that the wildest chimeras in those books of chivalry with which Don Quixote's library was furnished, would be found to have a close connection with ancient mythology." In his *Observations,* Thomas Warton noted that Milton read romances in his youth, and suggested that such books "were the source from which young readers especially, in the age of fiction and fancy, *nourished the* Sublime. I own indeed, that Milton's strong imagination might receive peculiar impressions from this sort of reading." Chaucer was introduced for further support and confirmation: "His old manners, his romantic arguments, his wildness of painting, his simplicity and antiquity of expression, transport us into some fairy region, and are all highly pleasing to the imagination."[9]

Many of these propositions owed something of their vitality to the historical premise that underlay them: that the imagination declines with the growth of reason and civilization. Even Lowth, who did not speak specifically of the English tradition in his *Lectures,* favored a conception of nostalgic primitivism: the notion that an unduly polished society is inimical to a boldly imaginative poetry of fine fabling. Thomas Warton stated the matter in a way agreeable to almost all. After the age of Elizabeth, he commented, anticipating Matthew Arnold, "prose became the language of poetry."[10]

Yet such exuberant celebrations of the reign and dominion of fancy encountered one particularly vexing problem. A wide-ranging appeal to human emotions implied that the cultivation of feeling offered an index to human nature, offered a most reliable way of measuring the vitality of the age and the literature it produced, and implied further that the progress of civilization was hostile to the higher flights of the imagination. Paradoxically, cultural primitivism was allied not only with a greater scope of feeling but with a greater nicety as well. Tender and pathetic emotions were as much a function of fine fabling as was the sublime. It was easy to conclude that through the cultivation of feeling, man could be restored to certain true and necessary realities of his nature that the progress of reason had closed to him.

Moreover, the more vigorously the poet's imagination acted upon his subject, the more likely he was to arouse and enchant the imagination of his reader. Both the tradition of empirical psychology, deriving from Hobbes and Locke, and the Platonistic tradition, stemming from the seventeenth-century Cambridge divines, contributed to the importance of the immediately affective. In the new Lockean psychology, as Ernest Tuveson has said, "the stronger the sense impression, the less immediately obvious its intellectual connections, the deeper it penetrates into the depths of the mind and the more likely it is to evoke a meaning which lies outside the scope of the understanding."[11] Quite some time ago Clarence Thorpe had noted similarly that Hobbes "furnished a powerful precedent for emphasis on effects by . . . psychologically inclined critics,"[12] among whom he included Dryden, Dennis and Addison, and among whom should also be numbered Charles Gildon. In the early years of the eighteenth century, however, the single most important exploration of this topic was conducted by Addison in *Spectators* 416 to 421, and his essays were to have considerable consequence among the mid-century critics.

In the several essays that comprise the second half of the papers on the "Pleasures of the Imagination," Addison assigned that faculty three distinct functions. It is first a *selective* faculty, a purpose that elevates the imagination through association with Bacon's theory of ideal imitation. Bacon had called poetry "feigned history," and commented on the ability of the imagination to "join that which nature hath severed, and sever that which nature hath joined." Furthermore the "use of this feigned history hath been to give some shadow of satisfaction to the mind of man in those points wherein the nature of things doth deny it." For Bacon imagination was the poetical faculty, as memory was the historical faculty, and reason the philosophical one. The purpose of the imagination was to provide not literal truth but illuminations of a kind unknown to readers of history or philosophy. Fancy could serve the purposes of truth, but generally only as subordinate or ancillary. As Hobbes also noted: "sometimes the understanding have need to be opened by some apt similitude; and then there is much use of Fancy." Metaphor, however, was not admissible where strictly truthful inquiry was the professed goal: "But for metaphors, they are in this case utterly excluded. For seeing they openly profess deceit; to admit them into counsel, or reasoning, were manifest folly."[13]

To Addison the particular value of aesthetic representation resided in the fact that mind searches for perfection, and perfection must be supplied by the mind itself. Art therefore mends or improves nature, presenting scenes and objects perfect beyond those provided by nature. This conception, derived from Bacon, represents the combined activity of two distinct faculties called by Dryden *fancy* and *imagination*. Dryden had assigned "invention" to the imagination, charging fancy with the responsibility for providing images and ornaments, adornments and embellishments for the inventive imagination. Addison, however, combined fancy and imagination into a single capacity and made no distinction between them.

In *Spectator* 416 he proposed that the poet "seems to get the better of Nature," and the idea is further developed in the suggestion that "Words, when well chosen, have so great a Force in them, that a Description often gives us more lively Ideas than the Sight of Things themselves."[14] The "lively" ideas of the thing, the impressions it makes upon the mind, imply the superiority of art to nature. But, in any event, art is a surrogate creation, something at least offering a pleasure similar to that derived from scenes and objects in nature. Addison avoids any implication that art is a feigning or falsehood. On the contrary, art conveys its own truth, one that is more lively, affecting the mind far more vigorously than do similar impressions derived from nature.

His terms insist upon a particular kind of appeal characteristic of art and different from that of nature. The impressions communicated by works of art, measured against the common standard of "lively," suggest the greater vitality of aesthetic objects. It may seem that Addison's artist functions as an illusionist, but this conclusion is inexact. Addison thought of the artist as quickening the mental processes of the reader by bringing objects to the attention of the imagination in a new way. Thus he justified novelty. Included in Addison's idea of the artist, however, are two principles of imitation that guide him. The artist is selective, taking from nature what he needs and neglecting nature's abundance, its excess, where it does not serve his purposes. Secondly the artist is more comprehensive than nature, adding to nature what is necessary to arouse in the reader (or viewer) more complex ideas (images) than are apt to be found in nature.

But in explaining the varying responses of readers to the same scenes and objects, Addison was unwilling to allow the difference to reside wholly in the subjectivism of individual readers or viewers. Judgment must be "discerning."[15] In one sense the conclusion is merely conventional, a familiar acknowledgment of the judgment's customary critical function. Judgment is called in to pronounce upon the integrity of the poet's work, the agreeableness of its order, and the fidelity of its parts to the whole. However, Addison employed the judgment as an agent of the imagination; the understanding, which he distinguished from judgment, is an agent of reason. Judgment evaluates the work as, to use a modern term, a heterocosm, and with such an enterprise the understanding has nothing to do.

In *Spectator* 417 the distinction is furthered: "A Poet should take as much Pains in forming his Imagination, as a Philosopher in cultivating his Understanding." The poet must gain "a due Relish of the Works of Nature."[16] The imagination is thereby anchored in nature, making nature the material ground of the poet's creation, and pointing toward the poet's responsibility to it. At first glance the conclusion to this paper seems to have little purpose in forwarding the argument, but Addison's discussion of Homer, Virgil, and Ovid, and the particular poetic province of each, prepares, through the reference to Ovid, for the later introduction to the "fairy way" of writing and to Shakespeare's "noble Extravagance of Fancy." Parenthetically, we may observe that as Addison progressed through the papers the "uncommon" mutates into the "strange," signifying that it is not mere novelty or variety that he had finally in view.

All that Addison had so far offered is prelude to his discussion of the "fairy way" of writing, his most venturesome defense of that which deviates from nature or common reality. His justification for this *way* is based primarily upon the validity of strong affective appeal, but deviations from nature, sanctioned in the preceding paper, are gathered up and brought to bear on the subject of *Spectator* 419. Addison here encouraged something like a natural supernaturalism, descriptions and representations of that which is not in nature but which is so presented by the artist as to fall in with "our natural prejudices." The proper referent is the "lively ideas" of *Spectator* 416: an interior reality formed of superstition and fable, existences within the imagination dating from childhood and part of common human nature. Descriptions so derived raise a pleasing kind of horror through "strangeness" and "novelty." They resurrect in the memory stories of the past "and favour those secret Terrours and Apprehensions to which the Mind of Man is naturally subject."[17]

The secret terrors latent since childhood open a road back to the closed past, to the buried life that lies within the adult. Tuveson suggests that Addison's argument here approaches pure aestheticism,[18] but as in Dryden's *Essay of Dramatic Poesy,* the term *nature* carries the freight of critical valuation. If by pure aestheticism one means a fictive creation having little or no relation to belief, then Addison's purposes are very different from what Tuveson implies. *Spectator* 419 puts us more in touch with Addison's conception of the imagination than do any of the other papers, probably because what the understanding must recognize as a weak delusion, not to be credited, the imagination regards as a responsible desire of the mind. For Addison one function of the imagination was to explore areas of experience which are closed to the understanding, areas which that faculty would necessarily dismiss as fictions of the mind. As did Dryden in the *Essay,* Addison shifted the burden of his argument from nature to human nature, such a shift being a familiar strategy of psychologically inclined critics.

The "fairy way" of writing is thus not merely a source of vivid impressions—and thereby the means by which, through the associational process, new experience may be created—but also a way of arriving, as it were, at *old* experience, that which in the adult consciousness lies buried in the lowest stratum of memory. The artist gives features to aspects of human identity otherwise inaccessible, and those poetic licenses and liberties that pass beyond the jurisdiction of the understanding are purposeful. Such representations are founded on a paradox within *nature:* the two-fold bearing of the term on mind and matter. Somewhat later, as though anticipating Johnson, Addison brought the two referents together by observing that in Shakespeare all nature is to be found, and Shakespeare is called upon to verify the uses of the natural supernatural. The probable and the marvelous are conjoined: "if there are such Beings in the World [i.e., *unnatural* beings], it looks highly probable they should talk and act as he has represented them." Poetry "has not only the whole Circle of Nature for its Province, but makes new Worlds of its own, shews us Persons who are not to be found in Being, and represents even the Faculties of the Soul, with her several Virtues and Vices, in a sensible Shape and Character."[19] The conclusion of *Spectator* 419 fully separates the imagination from the understanding, defines the province of the former, and sets forth a justification for the imagination as well as it was to be done in eighteenth-century criticism.

Spectator 420 proceeds boldly on the bases that have been established. The pleasures of the imagination are affiliated with the task of the historian and extended into the domain of the new philosophy. This constitutes a raid on the province of the understanding, qualified only by the distinctions which conclude the essay specifying what belongs properly and exclusively to the understanding. And in the last paper of the series, Addison restored the relation between the two faculties, asking his readers to approve metaphor and literary allusion, even in works designed to appeal primarily to the understanding, as "Tracks of Light in a Discourse."[20] Like moments of comedy in tragedy, the illuminations of the imagination in a serious discourse are complementary rather than disruptive. The imagination thus modifies the discursive severity of the understanding, lending to it colors not properly its own but which are in effect a graceful dress of thought. The suggestion is of one power lending illumination to another. Neatly and almost retributively the imagination is offered again as ancillary to the understanding, a tactful concession provided as compensation for the suspension of the understanding advocated earlier in the "fairy way" of writing.

With quite remarkable civility Addison mediated between the imagination and the understanding, defining and distinguishing the purposes and powers of each. In the process he outlined as the province of the imagination areas of experience that were not lost upon the mid-century poets and critics. It was to Addison that they frequently returned; he remained a master light of their seeing and a critical authority second to none for the licenses with which they sought to invest the imagination.

By 1711 the psychological tradition in English criticism, in conjunction with the increasing interest in the Longinian sublime, had made available to English writers a unique conception of the imagination. Restoration criticism had been highly attentive to the complex and vexed relation between the probable and the marvelous, a relation equally important to the critics of mid-century but one hardly tempered at all by moderate neoclassic principles. No Restoration critic seemed quite willing to sacrifice the probable to the wonderful or to disturb the balance which, it was commonly felt, should characterize their association. The moral and educative purpose of poetry, often expressed in the maxim that the duty of poetry was to please and to teach, remained primary.

When, however, the critics of mid-century revaluated the great writers of the English past, they tended to regard Spenser, Shakespeare, and Milton as poets with strikingly similar intentions, purposes which could be comprehended under the headings of fine fabling, of commensurately bold and figurative language, and of the direct appeal to the passions. Thus, while acknowledging their debt to Addison, they were inclined to emphasize not the cognitive value of poetry but its power to move and to affect the passions. By mid-century, moreover, the license for a broadly conceived appeal to the passions was drawing support not only from the reassessed English tradition but from such diverse sources as the Bible, Gothic and Celtic poetry, medieval romance, and from the conviction that the best poetry sprang from the imaginatively fertile conditions of cultural primitivism. Hurd, in his *Letters,* cited with approval Addison's essay on the "fairy way" of writing. Joseph Warton commended the "vigorous and exuberant imagination" sanctioned by Addison, and Hugh Blair, though acknowledging that "irregular and unpolished we may expect the productions of uncultivated ages to be," noted that they nevertheless abound "at the same time, with that enthusiasm, that vehemence and fire, which are the soul of poetry."[21]

Addison's papers offered justification for an enlarged understanding of human nature served and gratified by the fairy way of writing. Perhaps most importantly, *Spectators* 416 through 421 opened the way toward a more universal poetry, a poetry not the product of epoch but of a fundamental impulse shared by all literature, and in this regard the essays on the English ballad "Chevy Chase" contributed to the same goal. Others forwarded the ideal. John Husbands was among the early eighteenth-century appreciators of runic poetry, finding in the literature of "those Nations that are accounted *Barbarous,* Poems that may vie with any of the Performances of *Greece* or *Rome*." Some of the same assumptions that informed the historicism of mid-century critics are to be found in Thomas Blackwell's view that it is not "given to one and the same Kingdom, to be thoroughly civilized, and afford proper Subjects for Poetry." A high civilization and the poetic marvelous were seen to be in inverse relation to one another, though Joseph Trapp attempted to correct this opinion by lecturing his readers on the misinterpretations of the classics to which they were heir. "The Moderns seem to mistake that Part of Epic and Tragedy which contains the τὸ ϑαυμαζὸν, or the *wonderful,* confounding the *wonderful* with the *improbable,* and using those two Words promiscuously. If it was really so, the τὸ ϑαυμαζὸν would always be faulty; for that is always faulty, which is improbable."[22] But for an age that did not believe in the Homeric gods, the marvelous could not be similarly evoked, and to the Augustan critics Spenser commonly offered the example of an English poet whose inventions passed the boundaries of credibility.

For an age conscious of its own advances in rationality, Homeric superstitions required an exercise of historical permissiveness, a modest condescension to the exploded fictions of pagan belief, something in the nature of a relativism of belief that could be extended to Homer but not to Tasso. He was, Trapp remarked, "too full of Magic, Enchantments, Machinery, and aerial Personages." And what was true of Tasso was even more true of Spenser, who was "still more remarkably guilty" of treading "almost perpetually upon enchanted Ground."[23]

The ideal for literature of historical specificity, of cultural particularity, was undermined further by the attributes generally imputed to the Bible. Husbands fell back upon the authority of Robert Boyle to argue that Scripture " 'not being written for one Age or Climate only, but for all Ages, Nations, Sexes, Conditions, and Complexions, 'twas fit they shou'd be writ in such a way, as that none of All these might be quite excluded from the Advantages design'd in them.' "[24] The Bible coupled sublimity with the unimpeachable truth of sacred word. In the Bible, as Dennis had said earlier and Lowth later, the marvelous was implicitly probable, the sublime not a deception of the passions but a revelation of divine reason. The tradition of Christian supernaturalism, of sublimity inspired by the enthusiasm for the divine, attracted some of the more able writers of the age. Dennis, who could not condone Addison's approval of "Chevy Chase," could enthusiastically enlist himself in defense of religious sublimity and like Addison after him prove an able champion of *Paradise Lost*.

Minor issues are sometimes revealing. Pope commented that "Homer has his speaking horses, and Virgil his myrtles distilling blood, where the latter has not so much as contrived the easy intervention of a deity to save the probability." Trapp, answering Pope's objection, noted that speaking horses and myrtle roots dripping blood are "wonderful, but not improbable: For our most ingenious Translator of *Homer* seems to be mistaken, when he asserts, that these were perform'd without the Interposal of the Gods." But Pope's own note to the *Iliad* suggests his uneasiness with the marvelous: "Would not one general answer do better," he remarked, considering the relation between the probable and the marvelous, "to say once for all that the above-cited authors lived in the age of wonders? The taste of the world had been generally turned to the miraculous; wonders were what the people would have, and what not only the poets but the priests gave them." To Pope recourse to the marvelous always suggested an unwelcome concession to the demands of the rude and uneducated. Thus Shakespeare's defects arose from appealing to the populace: "In tragedy, nothing was so sure to surprise and cause admiration as the most strange, unexpected, and consequently most unnatural events and incidents."[25]

Yet the marvelous remained necessarily an essential ingredient of poetry. Especially efficacious in communicating pleasure and rousing the passions, the marvelous provided not merely a flourish or embellishment but a grace so essential to poetry that its importance, its cultural centrality, seemed hardly confirmed or justified without recourse to the marvelous. The greatest of the English writers were all, each in his own way and according to the requirements of the genre in which he established his fame, masters of the wonderful. In the continuing revaluation of the literary past some accommodation with these poets, and their employment of this traditional element in literature, was mandatory. Curt Zimansky, however, has well observed that "few parts of neoclassical theory are as unsatisfactory as its attempt to deal with literary illusion."[26] The potent and living example of Rymer's criticism was always at hand to enforce the need for probability.

The concerted critical voices at mid-century represented, as we have seen, a deliberate reaction to neoclassical restraint. While Temple cautioned his readers that exposure to "the visionary Tribe of *Faries, Elves,* and *Goblins*" may leave "lasting Impressions" and so "disquiet the sleeps and the very lives of Men and Women,"[27] Addison's *Spectator* 419 condoned all those elements that Temple feared.

Addison's justification of those credulities that continue to inhabit the mind even into maturity was commensurate with the more widespread inquiry into primitive literatures. For some critics there seemed present the discernible notion that the primitive is not merely a historical fact but a continuing psychological reality, a persistent, if anomalous, requirement of the mind. To Temple fables and fictions are disquieting, but to Addison the opening of the buried past seems potentially salubrious, possibly a source of new knowledge, but certainly an expansion of the human spirit. His exploration of the moving simplicities of the old English ballad and his reason for so doing were not in the least incompatible with Blair's delight in the Ossianic poems.

The licenses offered by Addison were eagerly seized by the mid-century critics. Hurd did not hesitate to cite the "pagan fable and Gothic romance" as the "most alluring to the true poet," and the lure of the remote is a common theme in his criticism. Joseph Warton paused in his appraisal of Pope to ruminate on the distant past: "I have frequently wondered that our modern writers have made so little use of the druidical times, and the traditions of the old bards, which afford subjects fruitful of the most genuine poetry, with respect both to imagery and sentiment." Thomas Warton discussed the visionary and allegoric poetry of the Middle Ages, the romantic devotion of Gothic times, the splendor of the marvelous, and cited "that bane of invention, Imitation." He noted as evidence of the recent corruption of taste and imagination that "judgment was advanced above imagination." Hurd referred to the French dislike of Ariosto and Tasso, and observed of that nation: "Their taste of Letters . . . was brought amongst us at the Restoration. Their language, their manners, nay their very prejudices were adopted by our Frenchified king and his Royalists." Slightly later in the same work he castigated Davenant who "open'd the way to this new sort of criticism in a very elaborate preface to Gondibert; and his philosophic friend, Mr. Hobbes, lent his best assistance towards establishing the credit of it." Such criticism, he continued, "grew into a sort of cant, with which Rymer, and the rest of that School, filled their flimsy essays and rambling prefaces." Perhaps Joseph Warton provided the apotheosis of reaction, and it is likely that the best-known passage in the entire two volumes comprising his revaluation of Pope is to be found in the dedicatory pages with which the work begins: "The sublime and the pathetic are the two chief nerves of all genuine poesy. What is there transcendently sublime or pathetic in Pope?" The rhetorical question was intended to clinch the argument at the outset.[28]

These critics spoke against what they conceived to be the spiritually stultifying criticism of the preceding hundred years and against that poetry which, with some few and notable exceptions, they regarded as the expression of unacceptable and imported values. Their revaluation of the English tradition resulted in a curious compound: Shakespeare's noble extravagance, Spenser's fine fabling, and Milton's sublimity were enlisted to serve the purposes of a poetry that would delineate "unsubstantial things." Such great predecessors were found to resemble more nearly medieval romancers, legendary Norse and Celtic poets, and Hebraic bards than those distant Greeks and Romans. The mainstream of English literature—so they argued—had been subverted and required redirection into its proper channels. In this respect mid-century critics spoke with the intention of breaking down the conception of a distinct and unique historical age which it had been the labor of Restoration criticism to construct. As Earl Miner remarks, "To Dryden, the very object of mimesis has taken on a diachronic, historical dimension derived from changes in reality, or the perception of it, by an advancing science."[29] Underlying mid-century criticism, and given special voice by the Wartons, was the desire for a universal, hence more permanent, poetry; its general validity affirmed by its appeal to the passions. Even such writers as Lowth and Blair, who were not at ease with poetic improbabilities, sought a poetry of vastly greater emotional richness than they associated with Augustan literature. They wanted a poetry of primitive sublimity, of vivid representations, and evocative of strongly imaginative and emotive response. Involved in such a conception was an idea of universal human nature, a feeling, at least, that what was most vital and valuable in man's nature had been neglected or inhibited by the spirit of neoclassicism and Augustanism. Thus primitive poetry, whether sacred or secular, confirmed human dignity in a special and remarkable way.

With the Restoration a glory and a splendor had departed from English poetry. It was necessary to recreate the vanished grandeur by revaluating the native tradition in the light of a more universal conception of poetry than previous English critics had provided. The key to the revaluation was the role of passion in poetry. Dennis in 1704 had suggested that "as Passion is the Characteristical Mark of Poetry, great Passion must be the Characteristical Mark of the greater Poetry," by which Dennis meant epic, tragedy, and the ode. But where Dennis had noted that "Poetry is the natural Language of Religion," not all, or most, mid-century critics followed this line.[30] To the Wartons in particular, poetry was the natural language of passion and religious experience was only indifferently the subject of poetry. The Wartons thus moved toward a secularization of imaginative experience, toward a conception of the greatness and worth of the human mind independent of its religious dedication. In *Spectators* 411 to 415, Addison offered the ontological argument premised on aesthetic objects, but the Wartons here went their own way. In opening a path back to medieval romance, Thomas Warton was following a track analogous to the one traced by Addison in *Spectator* 419. The buried realities of human experience met, as it were, in the poetry of a remote past which a more decorous age had proscribed as barbarous and uncivilized. Warton, as we have seen, was careful to note that Milton had been nourished on the old romances, that Shakespeare was familiar with "obsolete literature," that Spenser had drawn his "largest draughts" from Chaucer, from "The Well of English Undefiled."[31] Tradition is the single subject dominating Warton's *History*. From the Gothic scalds descends an extensive lineage leading into "the supposititious atchievements of Charlemagne and King Arthur, where they formed the groundwork of that species of fabulous narrative called romance." From this tradition arose "the marvellous machineries of the more sublime Italian poets, and of their disciple Spenser."[32]

It has proven easy for contemporary scholars to under-

estimate the Wartons. Viewed in relation to the obvious critical centrality of Johnson the Wartons may seem to us obscure
antiquarians. But the mid-century renaissance in criticism,
for which they were mainly responsible, was supportive of
the major poetry produced in the last fifty years of the century prior to the emergence of Blake and Wordsworth. They
led the revaluation of English poetry at mid-century and
were among the first to pronounce upon, in widely accepted
judgments, the limitations of the English Augustans.

However, what ultimately vitiated their criticism was
explicit in the dilemma proposed by Thomas. His criticism
foundered in the conflict between the real interests of society
and the special purposes and licenses of poetry, between what
was necessary to create an enlightened and reasonable society
and the extravagance appropriate to fine fabling. As he remarked: "Ignorance and superstition, so opposite to the real
interests of human society, are the parents of imagination."
Yet the progress of civilization deprived men of those "ex-
travagancies that are above propriety, with incredibilities that
are more acceptable than truth, and with fictions that are
more valuable than reality." Clearly the probable nourished
values not merely different from, but opposed to, those sustained by the marvelous, and Warton found finally no way of
reconciling the one with the other. The nearest he ap-
proached to compromise was through "a sort of civilised
superstition," coincident with Elizabeth's reign, a "set of traditions, fanciful enough for poetic decoration, and yet not too
violent and chimerical for common sense."[33]

In their own way, the Wartons sought from poetry, as did
Dryden in the *Essay,* an image of human nature both just and
lively, an acceptable concord between extremes mediated by
the elastic conception of *nature.* The several orientations of
this vexatious term made for difficult accommodations. It
pointed outward toward empirical nature and inward to-

ward human nature, and through the new historical absolutism proposed by those critics I have been examining, toward a more historically capacious and various human image than the Augustan humanists were willing to accept. More than any other single factor, the new absolutism undermined the special historical character of the age that Restoration and Augustan critics labored to create. Dryden and Pope thought and spoke as highly self-conscious representatives of a particular historical dimension. Yet by mid-century the new historical man of Restoration and early eighteenth-century England was rejected by the Wartons, Hurd, Lowth, and Blair, who found in him a distorted and diminutive image of human sensibility.

The appetite for ideal representation haunted the imaginings of mid-century critics, who desired poetry not merely to awaken the passions but to apprehend them visually, as if through the magic lantern of poetry the entire interior landscape of the mind would be illuminated and the panoply of unsubstantial qualities comprising our humanity be made known. To put the matter in this way was to recognize that the wondrous subject was man himself, not God or gods, not antiquated fictions, but embodiments of powers hidden within man, his essential reality. This was demanded in the name—to cite the title of Hurd's *Dissertation*—of a universal poetry, a poetry of indistinct social bearing and indefinite historical relevance but universal in the sense of satisfying the one essential requirement, that of astonishing the imagination by revealing the powers hidden in the mind. Hence, Hurd argued that poetry "deals in apostrophes and invocations; that it impersonates the virtues and vices; peoples all creation with new and living forms; calls up infernal spectres to terrify, or brings down celestial natures to astonish, the imagination." The corollary to Hurd's poetry of the startled imagination was Blair's *"Poetry of the Heart,"* the

Ossianic heart "penetrated with noble sentiments, and with sublime and tender passions; a heart that glows, and kindles the fancy; a heart that is full and pours itself forth."[34]

Little that was first-rate could be sponsored by such criticism if only because its inherent tendency was retrogressive and its informing principle was nostalgia for a vanished past. In taking the passions to be the true and perhaps only subject for poetry, it found no necessary relation between them and a precise historical identity. Destructive of epoch, because epoch had been defined as destructive of true poetry, it offered instead an ideal for poetry independent of historical period, and—far more limiting—was innocent of a myth of human identity to which experience could be referred. It is important to bear in mind that the very special role of the poet suggested by Dryden, and further established by Pope after him, was that of the creator and guardian of the national consciousness. The common method of Dryden's historical poems was to suggest the precise frame of reference—historical and mythological—for those topical events on which he offered interpretive commentary. In the middle years of the eighteenth century some of the more important poets turned their attention to redefining the task of the poet. Such an attempt was the burden of Collins's "Ode on the Poetical Character," of Gray's "Elegy," of Thomas Warton's "The Pleasures of Melancholy," of Smart's "Song to David." The concentrated attention on the poet reveals the obvious: that mid-century reaction to the poetry of Dryden and Pope involved necessarily a reaction to, and substantial rejection of, the magisterial role of the poet as high priest of English culture. The most difficult task confronted by the poets of mid-century was that of reconstructing and reformulating a commensurately high idea of the poet's obligation. Despite Wartonian doubts about the achievements of Dryden and Pope this proved to be very difficult to do. And because it was not done, a further necessity pressed upon Blake and Wordsworth at the end of the century.

In his late edition of Milton's minor poems, Thomas Warton remarked: "Wit and rhyme, sentiment and satire, polished numbers, sparkling couplets, and pointed periods, having so long kept undisturbed possession in our poetry, would not easily give way to fiction and fancy, to picturesque description, and romantic imagery." As a fiction of the mind poetry assumes its special status, its social and historical obligations minimized, its pictorial and representational qualities strongly emphasized. Such requirements led naturally to the new importance of the ode. Lowth stated: "The Ode . . . strikes with an instantaneous effect, amazes, and as it were storms the affections." When the mid-century critics searched among the works of later seventeenth-century poets it was Dryden's "Alexander's Feast" that, more likely than not, they found the most satisfying of his poems. In coupling this poem with Gray's "The Bard," Joseph Warton accorded it the highest praise of which he was capable. "If Dryden had never written any thing but this Ode, his name would have been immortal, as would that of Gray, if he had never written any thing but his Bard." Edward Young thought Dryden's ode "inferior to no composition of this kind."[35] It is not therefore surprising that, with very few exceptions, the most notable poetry produced by Collins, Gray, and the Wartons found expression in this form and that within this form the passions became the new marvelous subject of English poetry.

3

Mid-Century Poets

However tempting, it would be less than accurate to attribute a new poetic to the criticism of mid-century. By and large the poetry preceded the criticism, but the latter accorded well with the new lyric and provided subsequent justification for it. Joseph Warton's *Odes on Various Subjects* was published in 1746, as was Collins's *Odes on Several Descriptive and Allegoric Subjects*. Gray's major odes, "The Progress of Poesy," and "The Bard" were printed by Walpole's Strawberry Hill Press in 1757. Gray had been writing odes as early as 1742, but his English poems did not appear in print until 1747. Both Wartons were precocious poets; Joseph's "The Enthusiast," written in 1740, was published in 1744, and Thomas's "The Pleasures of Melancholy" appeared in 1747.

This burst of activity, similar in coherence to the criticism of the 1750s and 1760s and related to it as practice is related to precept, furthered the reaction to Augustan humanism and to the poets of the first half-century. Gray, Collins, and the Wartons define a movement of shared and common poetic values at least comparable to that of the Romantic poets, and, as with the later poets, some of these writers were, or came to be, acquainted with one another. Collins had initially planned to publish his odes in the same volume with those of Joseph Warton, but the plan did not materialize. Thomas Warton also knew Collins, referring to him in a letter to Percy as "my friend Collins."[1] In 1753 Thomas published anonymously a little miscellany called *The Union*. In it are to be found Gray's "Elegy," Collins's "Ode to Evening," placed next to Joseph's poem of the same title, and several other odes as well as poems by Smollett and Akenside. Gray and the antiquarian Percy, whose *Relics of Ancient English Poetry* was to appear in 1765, were well acquainted, while Percy and Thomas Warton were correspondents for almost twenty years. Through their common friendship with Hurd, Gray and Thomas Warton exchanged two letters late in Gray's life. There is no evidence that suggests Gray was ever personally acquainted with either Collins or Joseph Warton, though Gray did refer to Joseph's "The Enthusiast" in a letter to his physician friend of similar name, Thomas Wharton, in 1744. Two years later, again writing to Wharton, Gray commented on the odes of Joseph Warton and William Collins: "Have you seen the Works of two young Authors, a Mr. Warton and a Mr. Collins, both Writers of Odes? it is odd enough, but each is the half of a considerable Man, & one the Counter-Part of the other."[2]

These writers, more than loosely affiliated through personal or indirect acquaintance and strongly associated through common poetic interests, comprise a curious movement in English poetry. At least two of them, Collins and Gray, were men of unusual poetic abilities. Collins, however, by 1750, at the age of twenty-nine, was descending into madness and the last ten years of his life were to be devoid of poetic production. The number of poems he wrote in his brief creative period was comparatively small, and of that number only approximately a half dozen odes may be fairly counted among his best works. Gray, recognizably a major English poet of the second half-century, completed only eleven important poems in English. Most of these were short compositions and only a handful extended to one hundred lines or more. A somewhat mechanical way of measuring Gray's productivity is to count the number of lines in his major poetry: some 995 lines in all, or slightly more than the average length of one book of *Paradise Lost*. Though he survived until 1771, his creative activity came almost to an end with the publication in 1757 of the two major odes.

Joseph and Thomas Warton were men of wide-ranging talents, descended from a famous father. The Reverend Joseph Warton was a critic, scholar, schoolmaster, and poet. Thomas, if we substitute professor for schoolmaster, was a man of similar achievements and tastes, though undoubtedly more of an antiquarian than his older brother and clearly also a more productive (and better) poet. Yet their best-known poems may be referred to as juvenilia. Thomas continued to write and publish poetry throughout his lifetime, whereas Joseph's creative career was largely, if not exclusively, confined to the 1740s. It seems fair to remark that the chief efforts of each were directed toward scholarship and to the preparation of notable editions of Virgil, Milton, Dryden, and Pope.

In surveying this group of poets we confront both misfortune and oddity. Recognizably talented, well known to their contemporaries, and capable of appealing successfully to a large reading audience, they, for various reasons, left behind a remarkably small body of poetry. Generally speaking the reasons are not hard to find, though Gray's desultory poetic career remained to his friends both an enigma and an irritation. First of all, to continue to speak of the poets as a group, they were committed to a poetry largely in accord with conceptions of the fancy about which I have already spoken. In practice this meant a poetry of strongly figurative language, of bold and striking imagery, occasionally recondite, as in Collins's "Ode on the Poetical Character" and in Gray's "The Progress of Poesy" and "The Bard." Secondly, the delineation and representation of the passions, acknowledged as a major purpose of the lyric poem, resulted in a highly pictorial poetry, one that accorded well with Thomas Warton's re-

assessment of the Spenserian imagination. Spenser "bodies
forth unsubstantial things, Turns Them To Shape, and marks
out the nature, powers, and effects, of that which is ideal and
abstracted, by visible and external symbols; as in his delineations of Fear, Despair, Fancy, Envy, and the like."[3] Thirdly,
the representation of and appeal to the passions resulted in a
poetry of situation and event remote from common or conventional experience, common or familiar settings. The
fashion for cultural primitivism was engendered by the belief
that the great poets of the English tradition, as well as Celtic
and Hebrew bards, were uncorrupted by the progress of
civilization. Their imaginations were thus necessarily more
vigorous, their emotions more vibrant than those of the
over-civilized poets of the later seventeenth and early
eighteenth centuries. This conviction prompted something
of an affectionate turning to the presumed spirit and mood of
an earlier poetry, one considered more congenial both to the
high purposes of poetry and to the nature of man.

Thus, Collins's passions and Gray's pageants of the personified ills attendant upon human life were not a retreat into
mere antiquity but excursions into the marvelous and enchanted regions lying within the mind, explorations of those
uncharted territories in which the essential reality of human
life resides. Fancy dissociated from the restraints of the
judgment was to play the conjuror and to lead poetry into
areas of experience heralded by the fairy way of writing. It is
to the poets of mid-century we should now turn.

In 1743 Collins, after a juvenile flirtation with the eclogue
adapted to an oriental setting, published "An Epistle: Addressed to Sir Thomas Hanmer, on his edition of Shakespeare's Works." The "Epistle" is not only the first major
poem written by Collins but is the first important verse published by the group of mid-century poets. Though Gray had
already written his "Ode on the Spring," and Joseph Warton

"The Enthusiast," neither poem is quite as valuable for defining the incipient poetic given shape in Collins's "Epistle." It would appear that Hanmer's edition was undistinguished, though Johnson has later more than a few good words to say about it.[4] The poem itself has never enjoyed much esteem among students of eighteenth-century literature, yet in some very definite ways it not only presages the subsequent *Odes on Several Descriptive and Allegoric Subjects* but also organizes many of the poetic values with which the poets were to be occupied.

Like much that we have witnessed in the criticism of mid-century, Collins's poem defines an idea of poetic tradition, an element especially common to his poetry. The "Epistle" is a progress poem in that it traces the development of poetry from Greece to Rome to modern Italy to England, where in Shakespeare "Tuscan fancy" and "Athenian strength" are joined. In effect the tragic muse is linked with the Provençal muse of the melting passion; more specifically, the sublime and the pathetic are unified in Shakespeare. But such achievement is not sustained by Jonson or Fletcher, and the progress continues to celebrate later seventeenth-century French writers ("exacter France") but returns by line 75 to the "wilder . . . British laurel," to those "wreaths less artful [which] crown our poet's head."

The terms in which Shakespeare is celebrated are fourfold: he draws the "ruder passions"; he is "less artful" than the French; he brings the "historian's truth" (summoning lost manners, as recommended by Thomas Warton); he "bid[s] the manners live." Historical truth is joined to lively representation (just and lively images of human nature). The monarchs invoked somewhat more than halfway through the poem (Henry V, Edward V, and Richard III), in scenes suitable for painting, are illustrative of that union of the bold and pathetic previously cited by Collins. By setting out his images of the English kings, Collins implicitly defines the qualities he wishes a new poetry to bring into existence (or to recover). It should be more masculine than Fletcher's ("Of softer mould the gentle Fletcher came"), more artless than Jonson's ("Too nicely Jonson knew the critic's part, / Nature in him was almost lost in art"). It should contain that element of illusion that decks the masculine and the artless with the sweet cheat of Fancy's enchantment ("Where'er we turn [in Shakespeare's plays], by Fancy charmed, we find / Some sweet illusion of the cheated mind").

Feeling is embodied in the poem within a typological pictorialism derived from Shakespeare's plays. Antony and Coriolanus, for example, are types of particular passions. Thus, for Antony, Collins draws a scene from Shakespeare that might bear the title *Grief*:

> —And see, where Antony in tears approved,
> Guards the pale relics of the chief he loved:
> O'er the cold corse the warrior seems to bend,
> Deep sunk in grief, and mourns his murthered friend!
> Still as they press, he calls on all around,
> Lifts the torn robe and points the bleeding wound.
> (ll. 115–20)

For Coriolanus he paints the idealized picture of *Rage and Pity Contending*:

> See the fond mother midst the plaintive train
> Hung on his knees and prostrate on the plain!
> Touched to the soul, in vain he strives to hide
> The son's affection in the Roman's pride:
> O'er all the man conflicting passions rise,
> Rage grasps the sword, while Pity melts the eyes.
> (ll. 127–32)

Such scenes readily reveal their typological or allegoric qualities, and through them we come close to Collins's principal aesthetic conception: the delineation of types of feeling for which Shakespeare's tragedies exist as native sources to be mined for the properly *masculine* and *natural* emotions they contain. Dr. Johnson regarded Collins as a man "eminently delighted with those flights of imagination which pass the bounds of nature,"[5] but for Collins such delineations were the substance and essence of the *natural,* and in the "Epistle" he penetrated the recesses of human nature to represent pictorially those basic emotions he found in Shakespeare.

Jean Hagstrum, comparing Thomson's imagery with Collins's, observes that "Thomson's at its best arises from the vivid personification of *natural* detail and the organization of the scene around that personification, but Collins at his most typical personifies the *moral* and *psychological* abstraction and makes that personification central to the entire poem."[6] In this and other ways the "Epistle" is prophetic of the 1746 *Odes.* The scenes from Shakespeare are abstracted, as it were, from their dramatic contexts and translated, no other word seems quite right, into the rich pictorialism Collins desired. The idealization of Shakespearean scenes suggests the way in which the great English poet's art may be adapted to the purposes of the allegoric ode, how the *tradition* may be assessed for its continuing application to the purposes of mid-century poetry, and how Shakespeare's *naturalness* may be drawn upon to justify the special purposes of Collins's scenic and emotively oriented art. The "breathing nature [that] lives in every line" is the emotion resident in the recesses of the Shakespearean scene—that grief, that pity, that rage.

Collins held that Shakespearean drama is not, as Rymer understood it, a corruption of the tragic tradition coming down from the ancients but a continuation of it. The "speaking scenes" of Euripides' *Phaedra,* of Sophocles' *Oedipus,* are sustained in those like scenes found in Shakespeare's plays. Over the ages the moving art of the Greek dramatists reveals its affinity to that of the English bard. And as the "Epistle" progresses to its conclusion, the sister arts are revived by Shakespeare's store: "The sister arts shall nurse their drooping fires; / Each from his scenes her stores alternate bring." Literally, Shakespeare breathes into ("inspires") the arts of poetry and painting, kindling them anew, as "each beauteous image of the boundless mind" (Homer's and Shakespeare's, in this case) bedecks the sister arts and infuses them with truth and passion, with the truth that is in passion. In specific relation, moreover, to mid-century criticism, Collins locates Shakespeare within the Spenserian tradition; that is, within allegorical poetry, and the difference between the two poets is only one of genre.

All in all the "Epistle" suggests a quite remarkable adaptation of Shakespeare, revealing the same critical attention to those qualities of pictorial representation and appeal to the passions by which the mid-century critics were able to link Chaucer, Spenser, Shakespeare, and Milton. We could not expect to find a poem more in accord with the emergent critical values of mid-century. The nature that is in Shakespeare's dramas and celebrated by Collins is the continuing and living truth of human passions, truth that a merely ethical or didactic poetry (witness Warton on Pope) was in danger of neglecting and thereby losing altogether. In this regard the "Epistle" is a young poet's manifesto, a summoning of the values within the reassessed English tradition, a deployment of those images of feeling inhabiting Shakespeare's plays.[7]

Roger Lonsdale comments on Collins's odes to Pity, Fear, and Simplicity that all of them "deal with Greek tragedy to some extent."[8] In fact, however, that is exactly what they do not deal with. The references to Euripides and Otway, in the "Ode to Pity," provide a context of values largely irrelevant to Greek drama. The rivers Illissus and Arun, identified respectively with Euripides and Otway, suggest a continuity between Greek and English drama similar to what we have already witnessed in the "Epistle to Hanmer." The continuous element is pity itself, and the two rivers metaphorically define the flow of pity from Greece to Rome (as in a progress poem). More elliptically, if not more subtly, they suggest the natural element that is pity, the naturalness therefore of the pathetic mode.

Collins called the "Ode to Pity" a "rite," a ceremonial act invoking the goddess through the appropriate *signa* (the wren, the turtles, and the sacred myrtle). In the "Epistle" grief, rage, and pity are constituted scenically; that is, as the latent allegorical reality implicit in Antony's grief for Caesar, in Coriolanus's rebellion against Rome. In the "Ode to Pity," the personification is, as J. R. Crider points out, "no longer a means but an end, the focal point of the whole, invoked and supplicated as "'Thou,' an object which is also a subject and before which the poet feels himself an object."[9] Yet as Pity is a subject, a living presence in the poem, so, too, does Collins project himself into that presence and participate in the context that Pity inhabits. He will be her chronicler (provide the literary lineage for Pity), architect (build her habitation), designer (maker of pictures), and companion (he will live with her). In one sense Collins is making a poem about the properties associated with Pity (inclusive of the buskined muse) rather than writing a pathetic poem. Leaving aside the first stanza, the most conspicuous fact about the poem is that it is not pathetic at all. Collins is supplicating a creative ambience, the peculiar and particular one in which Pity resides, that is definitive of this poetic muse and which must be intimately known *before* one can write poetry.

The "dreams of passion" in which he wishes to "melt away" suggest a surrender to intoxication, to proto-Keatsian enticements. Collins is, however, far from mere languor; if anything, the poem celebrates energy evoked through association with the goddess. Pity's temple "Shall raise a wild enthusiast heat / In all who view the shrine," and "Picture's Toils shall well relate / How chance or hard involving fate / O'er mortal bliss prevail." It is energy that Collins wants, the energy that derives from intimacy with passion, the creative energy that goes into the making of a poet. The revelations of Pity that he holds out are in effect glimpses into the sources of poetic power, into the incorporeal, visions that animate and inspire.

In the "Ode to Fear," Fear is the quality "to whom the world unknown / With all its shadowy shapes is shown." Fear sees "the unreal scene," though Fancy mediates between flesh and spirit by lifting "the veil between." The insights define an imaginative reality in which, for example, Danger exists in the idealized and pictorial representations Collins provides for him:

> Danger, whose limbs of giant mould
> What mortal eye can fixed behold?
> Who stalks his round, an hideous form,
> Howling amidst the midnight storm,
> Or throws him on the ridgy steep
> Of some loose hanging rock to sleep.
> (ll. 10–15)

Vengeance is metonymously represented through her "red arm, exposed and bare." Fear is not only shown with "hurried step" and "haggard eye," but the feelings that have taken their toll on Fear are explained as well: "Who, Fear, this ghastly train can see, / And look not wildly mad like thee?" In the epode, Oedipus and Jocasta parallel the earlier allegorical representations of Danger and Vengeance. Fear's train includes Danger and Vengeance but also, in the material world, Oedipus and Jocasta, as though the latter are the physical embodiments of the former, of the spiritual realities Danger and Vengeance. Thus what is incorporeal has its bodily form (or at least reveals its effect on body), and the *reality* of Danger and Vengeance is confirmed by the experiences of Oedipus and Jocasta. As Collins says: "Thy [Fear's] withering power inspired each mournful line [of Sophocles' play], / Though gentle Pity claims her mingled part, / Yet all the thunders of the scene are thine."

The antistrophe defines Fear as the "spirit [who] most possessed / The sacred seat of Shakespeare's breast!" If Collins could feel as Shakespeare felt, then Collins would dwell with Fear. Both odes are about the writing of poetry; the "Ode to Fear" has to do in particular with the creation of scenes that extend the referential range of Fear. Thus Fear is associated with drowning seamen, with the tales of old bards, and with Halloween ghosts, but the overall effect of the poem is to supplicate topics that are fearful. Collins is almost saying that were he to write a fearful ode he would get into his poem the particular events and effects he mentions in passing. This of course is precisely what he does in the later "Ode on the Popular Superstitions of the Highlands of Scotland." What emerges, however, from the "Ode to Fear" are not merely the scenic elements which picture Fear or her associates, Danger and Vengeance, "gloomy Rape and Murder," but events or pseudoevents in which Fear displays the various modulations of feeling associated with her actions. To hear "drowning seamen's cries in tempest brought" is terrible, but different in effect from the ghostly legends of Halloween that "cottage-maids believe." The fluctuations of tone suggest that the purpose of the ode is to build up the complex, because various, affective presence called Fear. Throughout the poem Fear has been identified with Danger, Vengeance, Oedipus, Jocasta, Rape, Murder, drowning seamen, Halloween, and Shakespeare's tragedies. Some associations are presented more pictorially than others, but each manifestation extends the affective range of Fear. Through scene and through the poem's progress, continually including more manifestations of the fearful, an enlarged context illustrative of Fear is created.

In this way the poet brings into being qualities that, through the aid of Fancy, are made available to the imagination of the reader, and it would be hard indeed to think of a poetry intended to be more affecting than these odes by Collins. His odes are visionary only in the special sense that they envision through scene and allegory varieties of feeling associated with an emotion or quality. They sustain Hurd's remark that "fiction is the soul of poetry," and they duplicate the feat for which Warton praised Spenser, that of bodying forth "unsubstantial things." However, it was not fiction in which Collins dealt, for while the ghostly legends of Halloween are fictions of belief, they appeal nevertheless to the buried life within us and find their justification in the fairy way of writing.

Fear is, to quote from another of Collins's poems, one of the "shadowy tribes of mind." To provide local habitations and details, and by so doing bring into being members of this shadowy tribe, defines Collins's intentions in the odes to Pity and Fear. The descriptive is itself the allegorical, the latter made up of the descriptive particulars of which the poem is composed. Such images of feeling, however, are divorced from any referent larger than the emotion itself, and feeling remains somewhat tautologically the justification for feeling. Emotion does not find its rationale in a context that is illustrative of the occasion for such feeling, the needs that engender it, or explicative of the feeling as it bears upon the social identity of the poet. Augustan satire commonly locates the occasion for the poet's response in the behavior of his victims. The Romantic lyric often reveals response as a function of urgencies within the speaker pressing for resolution. Collins falls between these possibilities, and the compilation of a differentiated and varied range of feeling within the poem is sponsored by no identifiably objective or subjective fact. Fear simply exists; it exists as an accumulation of events that are variously fearful.

By keeping the reader concentrated upon emotion the poem virtually denies a larger application to which feeling may be susceptible. In the "Ode to Evening," for example, Collins seems mindful of the need for a somewhat larger reference for Evening's influence but locates this reference oddly enough in "Fancy, Friendship, Science, rose-lipped Health." The train of qualities, educed late in the poem, finds no special justification from the earlier events of the poem, and the affective presence of Evening is of such primary importance that the late appearance of its "influence" seems merely an additional grace provided to bring the work to its conclusion.

The passions are for Collins a sufficiently marvelous fact to command his entire attention. To derive influences from a natural fact may suggest Wordsworthian tactics, but the odd assortment of influences with which the poem closes implies only the conventional themes of retirement poetry, the consolations associated with the contemplative hour, with Evening itself. The appropriate tonalities commensurate with Evening are traced through the landscape, through Evening's "dewy fingers" and the "gradual dusky veil," and the fluctuations of description contribute to the creation of an objectified evening mood. It is, in eighteenth-century terms, tender and pathetic.

The "Ode to Simplicity" hardly requires extended treatment, for the familiar elements are again present. The descriptive terms that contain allusively a definition of Simplicity, the pictorial values, the familiar historical lineage, the justification for the relation between Simplicity and Truth, the decline of the arts, and the willing retirement of the speaker to some "temperate vale" provide the touchstones for the poem's meaning. The three odes, as they are about the poet and the writing of poetry, lead to the poem which culminates this progression within the volume, the "Ode on the Poetical Character."

Ricardo Quintana says about this poem that "Garrod was at least going in the right direction when he pointed out that it is really about John Milton." He adds, correctively, that the "poem signalizes not John Milton but rather the *Kind* of poetry—Sublime Poetry—that Milton created in *Paradise Lost*."[10] The poem begins in reference to Spenser, to the "Elfin Queen" who has blessed his "school above the rest," to the "magic girdle" which only one can wear, and to the right to wear it secured by "some chaste and angel-friend to virgin-fame." The metaphor associates a new poetry with virgin-fame, and having revealed to the reader the relation between magic girdle and virgin-fame, Collins halts his narrative to discourse on Fancy, to whom "the cest of amplest power is given." Fancy in turn assigns the "godlike gift" to bless "prophetic loins." The important elements associated with the gift are "visions wild" and feeling "unmixed her [Fancy's] flame." In other words, the visions wild are reminiscent of the natural supernaturalism evident in the earlier poems, whereas feeling "unmixed her flame" is identified with a poetical purity that is the analogue for chastity or moral purity consonant with Florimel, the "unrivalled fair" Collins derives from the third and fourth books of *The Faerie Queene*. Thus, putting everything back into its right order, poetic power is a gift from heaven, derived from Fancy, and presented to the poetically pure (the analogue also for virgin-fame) for the sake of sponsoring a new poetry in keeping with the character of old poetry ("blest prophetic loins"). The new poet is a new seer and his gift is divine.

As is usual with Collins, the first movement of the ode defines the historical justification for the values he wishes to introduce, in this case the values of Spenserian romance. The magic girdle derives presumably from Venus or Aphrodite and is therefore in analogical relation to the poetic power that originates in the first movement in Fancy. The second movement explores or investigates the origin of such power, or that band, that girdle. The band was woven on the day when God created the world and is consequently to be regarded as part of His original creation. But we learn further that Fancy ("the loved Enthusiast") is the agent of God's creation. Her act (breathing "her magic notes aloud") brings into existence the sun ("thou rich-haired youth of morn") and all his "subject-life."

Three elements exist prior to the act of creation: Wonder, Truth, and those "shadowy tribes of Mind." The latter enjoy some indistinct analogical relation to planetary bodies in that they move harmoniously in "braided dance," and it is probably exact to say that they are spiritual facts analogous to physical facts. Their braided dance is one of intricate relation or complex harmony. Like such shadowy tribes, Wonder and Truth are not created by the agency of Fancy but are powers quickened into characteristic action by Creation. Following the image of creation, Collins asks the crucial question: "Where is the bard, whose soul can now / Its [Creation's] high presuming hopes avow?" The reference in line 53 to "rapture blind" obviously prepares for the appearance of Milton in the poem. Clearly something of a Shaftesburian analogue between God and bard is suggested in the fact that God created with "thought," the bard "thinks"; but the bard thinks with "rapture" even as God creates through the agency of "the loved Enthusiast."

The complex progress of the poem attributes the facts of Creation to "fairy legends"; the story of Creation is a legend, one might almost say a romance, and thereby the stories of Creation and of the magic girdle are both placed in the category of fable. The magic girdle is invested with an antiquity as old as the world. It is fitting therefore that Milton, whose epic tells of Creation, should be the bard introduced after Spenser, as though there is some logical relation between the romance of Spenser and the epic by Milton, as though Milton *is* the bard who avowed Creation's "high presuming hopes." The relation between the two English poets is surely more complex, but it is relevant to that drawn between, say, Euripides and Otway in the "Ode to Pity."

The nature of the complexity is, in part at least, made apparent by the fact that Milton's sublime poetry is not merely a continuation of the Spenserian romance but a clear development from it as we move from romance legend to Christian revelation. Lines 63 to 67,

> I view that oak, the fancied glades among,
> By which as Milton lay, his evening ear,
> From many a cloud that dropped ethereal dew,
> Nigh sphered in heaven its native strains could hear:
> On which that ancient trump he reached was hung . . .

suggest the proximity of Milton to heaven, but line 74, "And Heaven and Fancy, kindred powers . . . ," observes the relation between creative powers that it has been the purpose of the poem to demonstrate. We should recognize, and will have further occasion to notice, Collins's concern with the relation between truth and fancy, or, casting the relation into the terms of the poem, between "fairy legends" and the revelation of "hallowed work," between fine fabling and truth, between Spenser and Milton and the development of English poetry. It would appear that Collins is decidedly not asking us to choose between two rival traditions but to recognize and acknowledge the proximity of Spenserian romance to Miltonic epic in terms of the poetic intentions and the ultimate truths that inspire each. As in the "Epistle to Hanmer," Collins's designs are critical, and the commentary implicit in both poems bears upon the ideas of poetic tradition within English poetry, with the ways in which a sublime poetry may be derived from alternate and yet similar traditions of romance and epic.

An "Ode on the Popular Superstitions of the Highlands of Scotland, Considered as the Subject of Poetry" (to give the work its full title) is the last complete poem produced by Collins, although it exists today with considerable lacunae in the text. Lonsdale dates the composition between November 1749 and early 1750 and adds that the Wartons, visiting Collins in Chichester in September 1754, saw the ode at that time. The poem was not published until almost thirty years after Collins's death, and the complicated history of the manuscript is detailed in Lonsdale's excellent edition. The poem does not represent a development in Collins's poetry, for in many ways it is perfectly consistent with the values of the earlier odes. But it is a full-scale commitment to the inspiration derived from primitive sources, and it is very easy to believe the Wartons were pleased with it. The highlands of Scotland provide the material for a particular kind of poetry which, though containing "false themes," may nevertheless be justified according to Addisonian principles and by the historical appeal of such materials. Quite clearly the ode is an excellent example, perhaps the best example in eighteenth-century poetry, of the fairy way of writing.

"Shakespeare's self," for example, found in the highlands "his Wayward Sisters," and such scenes, "daring to depart / From sober Truth, are still to Nature true," and "filled in elder time the historic page." Moreover, such truth is similar to that found in romance, in Tasso's *Jerusalem Delivered,* which Collins read in the 1749 edition of Fairfax's translation:

> How have I trembled when, at Tancred's stroke,
> Its gushing blood the gaping cypress poured;

When each live plant with mortal accents spoke,
  And the wild blast upheaved the vanished sword!
How have I sat, where piped the pensive wind,
  To hear his harp by British Fairfax strung.
Prevailing poet, whose undoubting mind
  Believed the magic wonders of which he sung!

(ll. 192–99)

The pathetic tale of the lost youth drowned by the malice of the "Kaelpie" or water-spirit suggests the embodiment in narrative of the values solicited in the odes to Pity, Fear, and Simplicity. Moreover, the ode relies far less heavily on personifications than do the earlier poems. Joseph Warton had termed personification "one of the greatest efforts of the creative power of a warm and lively imagination,"[11] but the "Ode on the Popular Superstitions" is more a demonstration of the poetic use that may be made of available primitive materials than it is an invocation of qualities in the *ut pictura poesis* tradition. It is also a full-scale treatment of values declared in the "Epistle to Hanmer," especially in the following lines of that early poem:

Where'er we turn, by Fancy charmed, we find
Some sweet illusion of the cheated mind.
Oft, wild of wing, she calls the soul to rove
With humbler nature in the rural grove;
Where swains contented own the quiet scene,
And twilight fairies tread the circled green:
Dressed by her hand, the woods and valleys smile,
And spring diffusive decks the *enchanted isle*.

(ll. 93–100)

Collins's critical intentions posited a return to the romance tradition and implied also the exploitation of native materials by which such a tradition might be resumed. However, as Arthur Johnston points out:

Romance was synonymous with magic, with the incredible and the impossible, with the abandoning of accounts of plain matter of fact,

in actions and character. . . . Most critics of the period were prepared to accept Homer's and Virgil's gods and goddesses, and the
epic equivalents of giants and enchanters, but were not willing to
extend the same charity to the romances. . . . The marvellous of
romance seemed more childish than that of the classics, mainly
because it survived in folk-tale and children's stories. It was rarely
combined with any deep understanding of human nature in the
probable parts of the stories.[12]

Yet if the marvelous, especially the marvelous of pagan
mythology, was not credible, it nevertheless contributed, in
Thomas Warton's words, "to rouse and invigorate all the
powers of imagination: to store the fancy with those sublime
and alarming images, which true poetry best delights to display." The opposing view was neatly expressed by Johnson where he minimized Shakespeare's employment of the
marvelous: "Other dramatists can only gain attention by
hyperbolical or aggravated characters, by fabulous and un-
exampled excellence or depravity, as the writers of barbarous
romances invigorated the reader by a giant and a dwarf." No
particular friend to Spenser, Johnson emphasized only the
instructive value of allegory, a merit to which Warton af-
forded no very high place.[13]

Not all the critics we have summoned were equally delighted by romance. To Blair the superiority of the Ossianic
poems was that his "heroes have all the gallantry and gener-
osity of those fabulous knights, without their extravagance;
and his love scenes have native tenderness, without any mixture of those forced and unnatural conceits which abound in
the old romances." Allegory often offered "shadowy Beings," fictions too intrusive and void of "that impression of
reality, which the probable recital of human actions is calcu-
lated to make upon the mind."[14] Yet whatever may seem
excessive to a modern reader in Ossian was referred by Blair
to the strength with which men in "the infancy of societies"
imbued their feelings and language, and while not exactly

encouraging fiction, he equated, as did the Wartons and Hurd, imaginative decline with the growth of civilization.

Some of the same objections evoked by romance were later provoked by the gothic novel. To one writer:

> Horror must be heaped on horror, and darkness thicken upon darkness, amidst cold clammy carcases, accumulated skeletons, blood-stained daggers, etc. Our prose must now *run quite mad;* mobs of metaphors, unlike similes, and ill-paired figures jostling and supplanting each other, must add *new terrors to the terrific* description. Nor must our brains cease to be racked for fine words, far fetched expressions, half concluded periods, and sentences breaking off in the middle.[15]

The objection, particularly to "far fetched expressions," bears heavily upon Collins's diction in the "Ode on the Popular Superstitions." Commonly in reading through the poem we come upon terms that found their first recorded use here: "unrustling," "fear-shook," "to-fall," or words that derive from Spenser's antiquated diction, which, to quote Johnson's ironic comment, is of value only "because it has been forgotten."[16]

Of the "Ode on the Popular Superstitions," A. S. P. Woodhouse concludes sympathetically that it "suggests indeed a whole new field of romantic poetry which Collins did not live to exploit."[17] Perhaps Collins would have so developed as a poet, but the "Ode" is in the pattern of the earlier *Odes on Several Descriptive and Allegoric Subjects* and is consistent with one kind of appeal to the passions and to the imagination. It is a narrative exploration of the values embodied in Collins's earlier poems, and only in this limited sense does it suggest a development of his poetry. Collins's madness came upon him when he was yet a young man, and it is both impossible and obviously unfair to predict the direction his subsequent poetry would have taken. Yet it is equally true that the appeal to the passions through the improbabilities of fine fabling, or the remnants of such elements, does not prove a significantly productive mine for the poets of the mid-century.[18]

The principal reason why this should have been so is readily at hand. While the psychological tradition in English criticism encouraged an emphasis upon effect, and often proposed strong impressions in the belief that their cognitive value was furthered by association, the revival of an allegoric or visionary poetry, replete with details of fine fabling, more often than not dissociated emotions from their immediate application to the ordinary terms of human life. The dissociation is neither incidental nor accidental; it is on the contrary a deliberate feature of the mid-century poetic. Having abandoned the immediately topical, as well as the deliberate social and cultural relevance that sponsored topicality, such poets as Collins tended to become isolated within emotion itself. To observe and reproduce the sublimity or pathos of human feeling is to move toward an art nondramatic and merely descriptive, one in which the objectification of the interior landscape of the mind is the poet's dominating motive. But the delineation of passion itself is an abstraction imposed upon human experience or, with equal justification, an extrapolation of qualities conceived as essential to human experience. In this scheme passion is essential; experience is what is stripped away, allowing the vital and permanent features to remain.[19]

Wordsworth was equally concerned with a poetry of permanence, but permanence was conceived by him to inhere within subject. For Collins permanence resided within passion, and passion was reconstructed as a visual object. Clearly, Collins was deeply concerned in his short-lived career with the task and purpose of poetry. Yet, as we are told at the conclusion to the "Ode on the Poetical Character,"

> . . . Heaven and Fancy, kindred powers,
> Have now o'erturned the inspiring bowers,
> Or curtained close such scenes from every future view.

It is no wonder that he turned then to Scottish superstitions as the subject of his longest poem, to an exploration of theme that offered no more contemporary relevance than did Gray's "The Bard." Both odes were the last major works by each poet; they did not signify new directions so much as they did the complete acceptance of the Wartonian ambience, the fairy way of writing, and the fine fabling that it had been the task of mid-century criticism to propound as the true, the fit, and almost the only, subject of a new poetry.

Collins's language further reveals the attempt to revitalize an antiquated diction in the service of a reactionary poetic. Commonly we find in his poems such lines as "With brede ethereal wove" ("Ode to Evening"); "In watchet weeds on Gallia's shore" ("The Manners"); or such expressions as "soul-subduing voice" and "viny crown" ("The Passions"); and "light-embroidered sky" ("Ode to Liberty"). His diction raises questions as to the particular kind of language appropriate for poetry, a lively topic at any time. In *Rambler* 122, Johnson defined the four qualities of style of which he approved. These were "pure, nervous, elevated, and clear." The first is free from "colloquial barbarisms, licentious idioms, and irregular combinations." The *nervous* is defined in the *Dictionary* as "well strung; strong; vigorous." Hagstrum remarks on it as follows: "A genuine virtue even though it could easily be vitiated by being associated with 'uncouthness,' the 'nervous' style arose from the imagination ('that energy that amplifies and animates'), from fidelity to nature (which produced 'liveliness'), from rhetorical emphasis and grammatical position, and from importance and dignity of subject matter." *Elevation* is the opposite of "low and familiar" words but also the opposite of "obsolete" and "peculiarities of phrase . . . remote from common use." *Clarity* is encompassed in Johnson's comment on obscurity, which "counter-acts the first end of writing," for "every piece ought to contain in itself whatever is necessary to make it intelligible."[20]

Johnson said of Collins in the *Lives* that his mind was "somewhat obstructed in its progress by deviation in quest of mistaken beauties," adding that "his diction was often harsh, unskilfully laboured, and injudiciously selected. He affected the obsolete when it was not worthy of revival; and he puts his words out of the common order, seeming to think, with some later candidates for fame, that not to write prose is certainly to write poetry." He refers to Gray's diction in the following terms: "There has of late arisen a practice of giving to adjectives, derived from substantives, the termination of participles; such as the *cultured* plain, the *dasied* bank; but I was sorry to see in the lines of a scholar like Gray, 'the *honied* spring.'" Almost all of Johnson's objections to the sister odes, "The Progress of Poesy" and "The Bard," have to do with language. In two sentences Johnson summarized his major objections to both poems: "These odes are marked by glittering accumulations of ungraceful ornaments; they strike, rather than please; the images are magnified by affectation; the language is laboured into harshness. The mind of the writer seems to work with unnatural violence."[21]

Johnson's remarks on style and diction could not conceivably be more opposed to the values celebrated by the Wartons and intruded by them and others at mid-century under the rubric of primitive poetry. To the mid-century romancers Pope was the somewhat suspect poet of elegance and refinement, but the Shakespeare of Joseph Warton's "The Enthusiast" "warbled his native wood-notes wild," while Thomas Warton's Spenser sang a "wildly-warbled song." Paul Fussell comments that for the eighteenth-century humanist the human psyche was still imaged in a very seventeenth-century way, "with 'will' in a position of almost military 'command' at the top, 'reason' or 'judgment' in the middle, and the senses or 'passions' as servants at the bottom." Aesthetic primitivism turned the order upside down. When Fussell reminds us also of the "dependence of the Augustan humanists on Shakespearian and Miltonic figures and motifs [as bespeaking] their close alliance with a conservative literary past, a past which is as justly termed 'Renaissance' as 'classical,'" we should remember further that it was precisely the conservative literary past, the Shakespeare and Milton of Augustan England, from which new and radical values were drawn.[22] While the Augustan humanists continued to find in Shakespeare and Milton support for their own poetry, the romancers were finding in the same writers the justification for a world of fine fabling. The humanists hoped to locate behind Shakespeare, steadied perhaps by Ben Jonson, a repository of classical values, or, at the very least, a repository of all *nature* in the senses in which Johnson employed that term in the Preface to Shakespeare. The romancers were discovering behind Shakespeare a naturalness inherently opposed to artfulness, a justification for their concepts of original genius and aesthetic primitivism, and an idea of Western poetic tradition that reached deeply down into the dim recesses of obscure medieval legend and epic. The mid-century critics returned to the springs of English poetry; at first this meant the return to, and reassessment of, Spenser and Shakespeare. It came to mean medieval romance, Celtic literature, Scottish legend, and Runic poetry.

Gradually what was being subverted was the Augustan proposition as set forward by Pope in the "Epistle to Cobham":

> Tho' the same Sun with all-diffusive rays
> Blush in the Rose, and in the Diamond blaze,
> We prize the stronger effort of his pow'r,
> And justly set the Gem above the Flow'r.
>
> (ll. 97–100)

Thus when Johnson spoke of Macpherson "abandoning" his mind to the Ossianic poems, and when he replied to Boswell's inquiry that such poetry could be written by many men, many women, and many children, his target was very clear. The Ossianic poems implied for Johnson ignorance, unsophistication, and mere spontaneity. Above all, their enthusiastic reception challenged the major humanist tradition descending from Greece and Rome and allied with Christian revelation. The Ossianic poems were gothicism redivivus. And if the humanists saw themselves as the inheritors of the only tradition that deeply mattered, they were confronted by the menace of a wider pan-European literature and challenged where they least expected to be by the radical redefinition of the great exemplars of English poetry, Spenser, Shakespeare, and Milton.

For Johnson to call Shakespeare "pathetic" was, Hagstrum observes, "to give him a cultivated Vergilian quality"; but Collins's conception of a *pathetic* narrative, such as was to be found in the "Ode on the Popular Superstitions," had no necessary classical antecedents and derived from a crude and fictitious fable. Moreover, even the sublimity of Shakespeare and Milton easily became for Johnson "a dangerous prevalence of imagination." The sublime was susceptible to the kinds of radical associations with which it was being imbued by mid-century and submits to two different interpretations: that of the rhetorically elevated and that which was identified with emotions of awe and grandeur. However much Johnson might approve the former, he was dubious of the latter as an element in literature:

That wonder is the effect of ignorance has been often observed. The awful stillness of attention, with which the mind is overspread at the first view of an unexpected effect, ceases when we have leisure to disentangle complications and investigate causes. Wonder is a pause of reason, a sudden cessation of the mental progress, which lasts only while the understanding is fixed upon some single idea, and is at an end when it recovers force enough to divide the object into its parts, or mark the intermediate gradations from the first agent to the last consequence.

Against Johnson's temperate distrust may be set a characteristic paean to enthusiasm by William Duff. Early poetry, "being the effusion of a glowing fancy and an impassioned heart, will be perfectly natural and Original."[23]

When Wordsworth, in the 1815 "Essay, Supplementary to the Preface," spoke of "treading the steps of thought," he provided a hint for understanding one kind of lyric form, particularly that associated with his "Poems of the Imagination." By that phrase Wordsworth meant to suggest a process by which the mind's orientation toward its object is increasingly clarified. The consequence of this activity is increased self-consciousness, its distant rewards are intimations, the acquisition of knowledge not previously available. Wordsworth's remark occurred after a brief review of the English poets from Shakespeare to Macpherson and after a comment on genius, which he defined as "the introduction of a new element into the intellectual universe." The new element is mimetic, not of feeling alone, but of feeling as it comes to be known to the mind observant of its own processes, of its own "steps."[24]

At this point a few distinctions are in order. Poetic theory of the later eighteenth century included a definition of the lyric as that which "has the poet's mind as its central source." Such a conviction, as eighteenth-century critics employed it, referred to the "'natural' and uncontrived emotions of the poet himself."[25] These "natural" emotions may be found in any number of middle eighteenth-century lyrics, most conspicuously perhaps in Gray's "Elegy Written in a Country Churchyard," and provide the reason for Johnson's commendation of that poem. Yet also involved in relation to the "natural" was the novel or new; the burden on the poet to speak a surprising truth, interesting because the truth communicated is familiar and yet not familiar,—what has been felt before, but not known to have been felt. Johnson, as usual, put the matter well: "The *Church-yard* abounds with images which find a mirrour in every mind, and with sentiments to which every bosom returns an echo. The four stanzas beginning 'Yet even these bones' are to me original: I have never seen the notions in any other place; yet he that reads them here, persuades himself that he has always felt them."[26]

Such a burden which was borne lightly by Gray in the "Elegy" normally pressed more heavily on the poets of mid-century. The odes of Collins and Gray move toward the quality of oracular discourse, toward a kind of enchantment of the imagination, a special sort of imagistic speaking by which the poet is relieved of the normal obligations of logic and syntax.[27] They suggest a romance element disciplined to the purposes of the ode, for which Tasso, Ariosto, and Spenser were the distant poetic authorities and for which Addison's papers on the "Pleasures of the Imagination" in conjunction with Shaftesbury's *Characteristicks* provided critical justification. As a prescription for poetry, make it new by making it old was never more keenly felt than by the English ode writers of the middle and later years of the century.[28]

It is under just such a burden that Gray labored, and his career remains perhaps the most puzzling to modern commentators on eighteenth-century poetry. It has become almost fashionable today to speak of Gray's public as distinct from his private poetry.[29] According to this view, the private poetry is good, is the real Gray, the Gray of the "Elegy," for example, whereas the public poetry is less satisfactory and betrays the corruption of Gray's talents. Even those modern critics who wish to praise him reveal an uneasiness with his poetry that perhaps derives from Coleridge's early objections

to Gray's "translations of prose thoughts into poetic language." Thus Spacks notices that Gray's images "often seem
inadequately felt," whereas for Doherty, "Gray is often misled by his creative impulse to fashion a fine image with not
much connective tissue joining it to its context." These objections coexist well with Matthew Arnold's explanation that
"Gray, with the qualities of mind and soul of a genuine poet,
was isolated in his century. Maintaining and fortifying them
by lofty studies, he yet could not fully educe and enjoy them;
the want of a genial atmosphere, the failure of sympathy in
his contemporaries, were too great. . . . Coming when he
did, and endowed as he was, he was a man born out of date, a
man whose full spiritual flowering was impossible."[30]

And yet one wonders. Never did a reluctant poet have
more congenial friends and sympathizers. Only in a very
special and limited sense did his "lofty studies" fortify his
poetry, for it would be more accurate to observe that such
studies freighted Gray's poetry with obscure references embodied in precisely those images to which Spacks and Doherty object. His images often suggest the effort to translate
historical reflections into their poetic equivalents, and as Gray
aged his poems were more grandly embellished with images
carrying the weight of an enlarged historical awareness. Thus
the peculiar effort of his later odes was to transpose history
and legend into the key of lyric poetry. Yet, even allowing for
modesty, it is not apparent that Gray's lyric gifts took much
possession of him. In 1757, in early middle age, he wrote to
his favorite correspondent, Wharton: "You apprehend too
much from my resolutions about writing: they are only
made to be broken, & after all it will be just as the maggot
bites." Again, a year later in another letter to Wharton: "I by
no means pretend to inspiration, but yet I affirm, that the
faculty in question is by no means voluntary. it is the result (I
suppose) of a certain disposition of mind, wch does not de-

pend on oneself, & wch I have not felt this long time. you that are a witness, how seldom this spirit has moved me in my life, may easily give credit to what I say." And much later, in 1768, he was making the same statement to Walpole: "If I do not write much, it is because I cannot."[31]

Although his letters to both Wharton and Walpole, and to others, were filled with references to books and authors and sometimes include parts of, or completed poems, there is very little reference to the thoughts or impulses that governed the writing of particular works. Poems were often begun, put aside, recommenced and finished, if completed at all, months or even years later. The process was casual, even desultory. Other interests or the pleasures of travel and visits intervened. Of the "two or three Ideas more in my head," to which he referred in one letter, only "The Bard" was ever to be concluded.

Without question, however, Thomas Gray deserves to be remembered as a major English poet of the second half-century. If it were only for the "Elegy" his reputation would endure, for it is surely the finest elegiac poem of the age and one of the half-dozen or so great English elegies. As was usual with Gray the poem's progress was hesitant and delayed (two distinctly different versions of the poem exist), and its publication imposed upon him when the poem was pirated from privately circulated copies and printed by *The Magazine of Magazines*. Its publication by Dodsley in 1751 places it somewhere more than halfway in Gray's poetic career, between the highly productive year of 1742 and the publication of the two Pindaric odes in 1757.

Almost everyone who reads poetry is familiar with the opening of the poem. It echoes lines from Milton and Shakespeare (and is echoed later by Beattie and Wordsworth); it reflects a melancholic evening mood that has probably never found better expression. The eye of the speaker moves along the periphery of vision and returns to its center, the church-yard where "the rude forefathers of the hamlet sleep." As the legacy of day is the night, the legacy of the past is death, an inheritance of mortality bequeathed equally by the rich and by the poor. Everyone awaits the inevitable hour. Within the poem the great brooding fact of the churchyard stands as an abiding memento mori, a powerful eschatological symbol appropriately heralded by the "droning beetle," the "moping owl," the "yew-tree's shade." Against such an initial vision, as its contrary, are set the emblems of Christian eschatology: the "incense-breathing morn," "the swallow," "the cock's shrill clarion," "the echoing horn"—all of which shall no more rouse the slumberers. The vast negative absolute of death informs the poem, and Gray confronts the omnipresent fact of mortality, letting the confrontation arise implicitly from the opposition of the two major symbols within the poem, the chronicle and the grave, the epitaph and the churchyard.

One of the abiding paradoxes of the poem resides in the idea of satisfactory unfulfillment: village-Hampdens, mute, inglorious Miltons, guiltless Cromwells of the rural life. The paradox is spawned by Gray's vision of human life as dominated by the only inevitability it contains, that of death. Before this fact the triumphs of man pass into the insignificance of a trivialized relativism, for the paths of glory, like all paths, "lead but to the grave." Against the grave is posed the chronicle or epitaph, and the latter is of considerable complexity in the poem. Its development is through various modalities before it emerges finally as the poet's own epitaph with which the work concludes. The specific manifestations of the chronicle include the "annals of the poor," the "animated bust," the "boast of heraldry," the "storied urn," the "frail memorial." In each case the objects of remembrance are minimized or diminished by the qualifying context: the annals of the poor are "short and simple," the boast of heraldry "awaits the inevitable hour," the storied urn and animated bust cannot "back to its mansion call the fleeting breath," the memorial is "frail." Such images enforce futility. Yet what emerges as truly valuable is human relationship. Gray's own reading of epitaphs is a coming-to-know; that is, he did not know these people as they lived; he knows them by the imaginative recreation of their lives through a meditation on the surviving memorials.

So, too, we are given to understand, will the kindred spirit know the narrator through his own epitaph. If in the end everyone is alone, solitude is qualified by the fact of a shared mortality, and further qualified by the presence of a kindred sensibility. Death is not rationalized in the poem; lacking a specifically Christian or neo-Platonic context it cannot be. But what are rationalized are the unselfrealized lives, of which the poet's life is one example. In this way the "Elegy" is perhaps most of all an exercise in the varieties of feeling: the speaker feels for the unhonored dead and for the honored dead; he imagines particular persons for whom he can feel; he employs the pathetic fallacy to feel for the flower "born to blush unseen"; he feels for "mankind"; and through the kindred spirit he feels for himself. It is an exercise in sensibility. The darkness in which the narrator stands is the night of mortality illuminated only by varieties of feeling. This common denominator of sympathy, as everything in the poem evidences, is all that binds man to man, and, along with the fact of death that occasions this sympathy, is the single principle of unity within life perceived by the poet.

However impressive Gray's achievement here, the poem is not the specially isolated example of excellence it is sometimes taken to be, and it offers no radical departure from the common mode of his earlier works. The "Ode on a Distant Prospect of Eton College" is rich in allegorical personages and in the range of feeling that informs the poem. So, too, in the "Elegy," do we find Ambition, Grandeur, Memory, Honor, Flattery, Death, Knowledge, Penury, Luxury, Pride, Science, Forgetfulness, Contemplation, Melancholy, and Misery. All are agents of human experience, peopling the poem as profoundly as they inform human life itself. Such excursions into feeling imply Gray's métier, the ambience in which he bodies forth "unsubstantial things," giving them a local habitation and a name and filling his poem discretely with sublime and pathetic emotions.

Gray's poetry seems to rely largely upon two modes as a function of meaning. In one, as in the "Ode on a Distant Prospect of Eton College," he magnifies, exaggerates, enlarges; in the other, as in the "Ode on the Spring," he minimizes, deflates, diminishes. In either mode a speaker views objects at a distance, and both "The Progress of Poesy" and "The Bard" are grander arrangements of that distancing which Gray's temperament, as much as his talent, led him to employ. Unlike many of his contemporaries he was seldom a descriptive or landscape poet for more than a few lines consecutively and was quick to move into the reflective mood that the context encouraged. The subjects to which he was attracted, moreover, almost all involved, either directly or by implication, a protracted span of time. As in the "Ode on the Spring," the first of his English poems, the immediate event is referred to its larger temporal significance—the life span of a man—and the event takes its importance from this reference.

In the "Ode on the Spring," Gray's procedure was to define a classically derived context, replete with echoes of Anacreon, Lucretius, Horace, Virgil, Propertius, and more modern poets.[32] Under the "broader browner shade" we overhear a reflective commentary on life's limitations, on the vanity and "ardour of the crowd," on the indigence of the great. Despite the playfulness of tone, the "Ode" is the "Elegy" in miniature, contrasting the hapless mass of humanity with the fortunate few. The theme of human vanity and the transience of life, the conventional counters of Gray's thought, run through the poem, and the fourth stanza rehearses those oppositions so trenchantly at the heart of the "Elegy": "they that creep, and they that fly" end in the nonbeing "where they began." Even the "poor moralist" of a speaker, so addressed by the "sportive kind" in response to his gravities, anticipates Gray's address to himself in the "Elegy." Such lines as "Still is the toiling hand of Care; / The panting herds repose" suggest the more famous opening of the "Elegy" but are here cast into the smaller metrical unit consistent with the ironic tone of the "Ode on the Spring."

Gray's tendency was to reflect on the diminished thing that is human life and to suggest, even where it was least expected, the elegiac mode. His elegiac ruminations, unlike those of Wordsworth, who often employed the same mode, were well described by William Shenstone's reference to the "truly virtuous pleasure connected with many pensive contemplations, which it is the province and excellency of elegy to enforce."[33] The "Ode on a Distant Prospect of Eton College," written several months later, again establishes favorite oppositions as early innocence is opposed to later experience. As in the "Elegy," Gray summons a host of personifications to establish the range and character of human ill, and specific though these ills be they are merely in generalized relation to the mind of the speaker. Jealousy has a "rankling tooth," Envy is "wan," Shame "skulks," Love is "pining," Infamy is "grinning," and so on through the dozen or more "ministers of human fate."

One of Gray's favorite methods, as in the "Ode to Adversity," was to create a personification and to surround it with subsidiary personifications. Thus, in the "Ode on a Distant

Prospect of Eton College," Misfortune has a duly enumerated "baleful train." So, too, is there a "painful family of Death, / More hideous than their Queen," comprised of Poverty and Age and others identified only as a "grisly troop." In the "Ode to Adversity," Folly is trailed by an "idle brood," "Wild Laughter, Noise, and thoughtless Joy." All flee before Adversity's "frown terrific," taking with them "the summer friend, the flattering foe" to be received by "vain Prosperity" to whom they make their vows "and are again believed."

The "Ode to Adversity" is in one way an answer to the Eton College ode and therefore another part in the puzzle of pieces leading to the "Elegy." For Adversity is evocative of the sympathetic imagination teaching Gray through misfortune, "What others are to feel, and know myself a man." Gray's incarnations resemble Pope's pictorializing in *Windsor Forest:*

> . . . *Envy* her own Snakes shall feel,
> And *Persecution* mourn his broken Wheel:
> There *Faction* roar, *Rebellion* bite her Chain,
> And gasping Furies thirst for Blood in vain.
>
> (ll. 419–22)

These lines are among the very few passages in Pope's poetry to which Warton was willing to accord the ultimate compliment, "genuine and sublime poetry." Gray's personifications suggest an intensification of this mode, a willingness to bring poetry as close as possible to the more immediately affective art of painting. While the principles of literary pictorialism constitute an awkward poetic, since in no way can a poem rival that companion art in which descriptive details coexist simultaneously, Gray's pictorialism leads toward a principle of structure evident in the "Ode to Adversity." An animistic nature is the product of the extended use of personification; derivative or secondary personifications provide the elements for the progress of the poem.[34] For example:

Scared at thy frown terrific, fly
Self-pleasing Folly's idle brood,
Wild Laughter, Noise, and thoughtless Joy,
And leave us leisure to be good.
Light they disperse, and with them go
The summer friend, the flattering foe;
By vain Prosperity received,
To her they vow their truth and are again believed.

(ll. 17–24)

These figures are immediately succeeded by the introduction of Wisdom, Melancholy, Charity, Justice, and Pity. They constitute another area of the general scene, extending the affective range of the poem through pictorial effects (Melancholy is a "silent maid" with "leaden eye," etc.) and filling in the associations which normally cluster about the principal figure of Adversity. The poem itself is a kind of ideogram, or extended image, presenting the idea of Adversity by summoning all those qualities attendant upon it. Literary pictorialism was commonly associated with clear and distinct ideas, but it was equally common for writers of the period to remind their readers, as David Hartley did in 1749, of the greater vividness with which painting can communicate ideas.

Exactly like Locke before him, Hartley held that "the ideas of sight are the most vivid of all our ideas, and those which are chiefly laid up in the memory as keys and repositories to the rest."[35] Beginning with line 35 in the poem what might be called the negative image of Adversity, the guise in which she is requested not to appear, is created by Gray. He thus paints two pictures of Adversity—one in which he implores her not to appear, but the other, commencing with line 41, in which she is invited to come forth. If Gray was thinking of poetry as painting, as he undoubtedly was, he gained an advantage by the double images of Adversity which eighteenth-century readers would have been quick to recognize.

The characteristic progress is further revealed in the fragment "Ode on the Pleasure Arising from Vicissitude." The meditations on man (lines 23ff) give rise to the almost identical personified pageant. Misfortune, Reflection, Sorrow, Hope, Pleasure, Grief, Misery, Comfort, all make an appearance as the sum of possibilities comprising the figure Vicissitude. The processional mode is so common a feature of Gray's work, and so often limits the exploration of theme, that the "Elegy" seems all the more remarkable within Gray's canon. On the other hand the reappearance in the poem of features common to Gray's poetry reinforces the coherence of his work between 1742 and 1754 or 1755 when "Vicissitude" was written. The mixed character of human life, vicissitude itself, is regarded advantageously by the poet and leads into the moral reflection with which the poem closes.

All in all, the theme of human limitation strongly informs Gray's poetry and suggests the attractiveness of the elegiac mode to him. To juxtapose him to Wordsworth at the end of the century would do neither poet a disservice, but to do so suggests the paradox of middle and later eighteenth-century poetry. There were few religious poets of importance; there were equally few secular poets of major achievement. Isolated not in his age but rather within the conventions of a mid-century poetic, Gray failed to be the major voice of his time that the "Elegy" promised. He found within the theme of human limitation only a weakly realized sympathetic imagination, and his poetry falters in the mere glimpses of appalling human ill to which he returned again and again.

"The Bard," along with "The Progress of Poesy," was held in high critical esteem in the second half-century despite the obscurity to which many readers objected. Here it is useful to turn briefly to Johnson's "Vanity of Human Wishes"; from Johnson's purposes in this poem we may inferentially derive the grounds of his objection to "The Bard."

The "Vanity" offered authentic history; that is, it employed various historical personages in the service of a moral idea. It was a product of the humanistic tradition that descended, within the boundaries of neoclassic thought, from Dryden through Swift and Pope to Johnson and to the Goldsmith of "The Deserted Village" and "The Traveller." "The Bard" offered not history but fable; Gray's intention was to dramatize the visionary power of the primitive Welsh poet. In Johnson's poem history is ceaseless replication, resulting in the submergence of heroic action within a philosophy of human limitation. One of Johnson's purposes was to render acceptable to the reader his own subjection to time, and to those duplications of the past in the present, which end finally within the individual life in the ultimate duplication, that death which comes to all men.

Johnson's sense of history rationalizes providential dispensations, transmuting death into "kind Nature's signal of retreat," and invoking, in conclusion, "celestial Wisdom." To recognize the latter is the purpose of life; it is an intelligent and pious recognition justified by the unchanging conditions of human life as those conditions are manifest in history. The optimism evident in the poem is born of restricted possibility; the human condition is rooted in the human past, and man is the comforted, though not wholly comfortable, recipient of what is quintessentially true of human life. Johnson so organizes his extensive view as to compose a drama of historical personages. He employs his historical sense to normalize the radical tendencies of man and to return both poet and reader to the center of their cultural values. In sum, he puts the reader in touch with what is historically and therefore experientially authentic and reliable, probable and wonderful simultaneously. The authority for the great normative historical vision, descending from Greece and Rome and manifest in the greatest of the English writers, is located in its essential reality. It is the intelligible world of causes and consequences that remains fundamentally undisturbed by process or change, and the values of its relevance to the present are immediately apparent from Dryden's "Absalom and Achitophel" to Akenside's "Epistle to Curio." The various personages of the "Vanity" arise from the ground of a complete, coherent, and fulfilled world of experience.

"The Bard" incorporates a different conception. Of the poem Johnson remarked: "To select a singular event, and swell it to a giant's bulk by fabulous appendages of spectres and predictions, has little difficulty, for he that forsakes the probable may always find the marvellous." When Boswell wrote to Joseph Warton in March 1790, his *Life of Johnson* was already in the press. Yet he asked of Warton: "If you can recollect the origin of Johnson's prejudice against Gray's poetry, pray let me have it." Warton answered that Johnson's "strange aversion to Gray's poetry" arose from Johnson's taste for "that sort of poetry, that deals chiefly, in nervous, pointed, sentimental, didactic Lines." Warton's response, however, does not accurately measure Johnson's dislike for Gray or his poetry. That Johnson disliked Gray as timid, reclusive, and somewhat self-indulgent we may fairly surmise. That he disliked Gray's poetry on other grounds we know. For Johnson, "The Bard" is a "revival [which] disgusts us with apparent and unconquerable falsehood. 'Incredulus odi.'"[36]

In the light of Gray's earlier poetry, in view especially of the "Elegy," "The Bard" seems initially a suprising poem for him to have written. It may be that it early expressed his interest in old Norse and Welsh poetry, an interest that was to reach a climax in his proposed but abandoned history of English poetry and in the three Norse and Welsh "translations" of 1760–1761. It was in any event the kind of poetry in which the Wartons delighted. Joseph Warton concluded his two-volume study of Pope by noticing that Pope "has written nothing in a strain so truly sublime, as the *Bard of Gray*." What Warton and most of his age found to praise in the poem is evident in Addison's discussion of the fable in *Paradise Lost*: "The great Secret therefore of Heroic Poetry is to relate such Circumstances, as may produce in the Reader at the same time both Belief and Astonishment. This is brought to pass in a *well chosen* Fable, by the Account of such things as have really happened, or at least of such things as have happen'd according to the received Opinions of Mankind."[37]

Earlier in his discussion Addison had said that "the Fable should be filled with the Probable and the Marvellous." Of "The Bard" we know from its "Advertisement" that it was "founded on a tradition current in Wales," and we know also that Gray's source for this tradition was Thomas Carte's *General History of England*. Carte's source in turn was Wynne's *History of the Gwedir Family,* and the tradition mentioned by Wynne was apparently verified by Evan Evans, the Welsh scholar, in correspondence with Thomas Percy as, at the very least, a tale having its basis in Welsh legend.[38]

In Warton's long study of Pope's poetry there was no poem he appreciated more than "Eloisa to Abelard." Of the two lovers he stated: "Their distresses were of a most Singular and Peculiar kind; and their names sufficiently known, but not grown trite or common by too frequent usage." Eloisa and Abelard provided the basis for a distressing tale founded in fact but nevertheless "singular and peculiar." More specifically, however, Eloisa herself was the center of Warton's interest: "I now propose to pass through the Epistle in order to give the reader a view of the various turns and tumults of passion, and the different sentiments with which Eloisa is agitated."[39] This for Warton was the real subject of the poem, even as the "various turns and tumults of passion" provided the real subject of the "The Bard."

After imagining the "wretched old man . . . on the top of a rocky eminence," he further elaborated the character of the passions possessing him:

At sight of the bloody chiefs, he instantly breaks out into abrupt and various execrations. . . . But this sudden and most violent burst of anger soon gives place to a softer passion. He laments the untimely deaths of his friends and brethren, in words of the most plaintive tenderness, and most compassionate regret; till, by degrees, he is once more roused to thoughts of vengeance. He imagines that the ghosts of the murdered bards stand present at his call. He weaves, with horrid rites, the destiny of Edward; and denounces misery and affliction on all his race. Again his mind is calmed: he directs his prospect still farther into futurity; and, after soothing his despair, by a survey of happier times, and more merciful princes, throws himself from the rock, with a kind of sullen satisfaction, into the flood below.[40]

To Warton, Pope's Eloisa and Gray's bard offered the experience of passion unparalleled within the poetry of either writer, and he dismissed as without thematic purpose "any, or all, of those historical portraits, which are painted in such animated colours through the piece."[41]

Generalizing on Pope, Warton concluded that his reputation "among posterity will be principally owing to his *Windsor Forest,* his *Rape of the Lock,* and his *Eloisa to Abelard;* whilst the facts and characters alluded to and exposed in his later writings, will be forgotten and unknown, and their poignancy and propriety little relished. For Wit and Satire are transitory and perishable, but Nature and Passion are eternal."[42] The terms *nature* and *passion* were for him as nearly synonymous as were *wit* and *satire.* In this context, nature found its referent in the varied sentiments, sublime and pathetic, with which character is endowed, sentiments "singular and peculiar" owing to an unusual episode and its effect upon a character of strong sensibility.

For readers in the middle years of the century "The Bard" was the apotheosis of the sublime ode, "so wildly awful, so gloomily terrific."[43] Strictly speaking it was not a religious poem, but its affinities with the Hebraic prophetic poem, its high theme of the destiny of kings, and the vengeance supernaturally visited upon Edward's descendents fulfilled all the most lofty requirements of sublimity. Moreover "The Bard" deserved a prominent place in the tradition of the sublime ode descending from Dryden. In his edition of *Dryden's Poetical Works* Joseph Warton observed that "if Dryden had never written any thing but this Ode [i.e., "Alexander's Feast"], his name would have been immortal, as would that of Gray, if he had never written any thing but his Bard." He noticed especially "the succession of so many different passions and feelings," and his note to the poem continued to relish and elaborate upon the various passions which the poem presents. He objected, as might be expected, only to "the epigrammatic turn of the four concluding lines."[44]

The three Norse and Welsh translations of 1760–1761 bear fragmentary testimony to the twilight of Gray's career. The romantic image of Gray poring over Old Norse and Welsh is sadly vitiated by the fact that he worked from Latin texts to produce a few Macphersonic episodes of little dramatic power. By this time Gray was reading Ossian and communicating an enthusiastic response to the coterie. Blair had superintended the publication of the *Fragments* and written the preface. Gray had seen some of the poems in manuscript, as had Walpole, and wrote to that connoisseur of being "charmed . . . [by] two specimens of Erse poetry." Two months later, to Wharton, he had "gone mad about them," was *"extasié* with their infinite beauty." To both Mason and Clerke in 1760 he admitted to being "more puzzled than ever about their antiquity, thought I still incline (against everybody's opinion) to believe them old."[45]

His own translations, "The Fatal Sisters," "The Descent of Odin," and "The Triumphs of Owen," are little more than a mere heightening of descriptive detail. Odin's horse becomes "coal-black," is ridden down a "yawning steep." Garm, the guardian of the underworld encountered by Odin in his progress toward the prophetess, has a "shaggy throat. . . carnage filled," and jaws that drip "foam and human gore." The prophetess is a witch from the landscape of *Macbeth*, and echoes of earlier English verse are drawn from everywhere, perhaps most conspicuously from Spenser. Norton Nicholls in his *Reminiscences of Gray* remarked that "Spencer was among his favorite poets, & he told me he never sat down to compose poetry without reading Spencer for a considerable time previously."[46]

From the 1740s to the late fifties and early sixties Gray moved from elegiac sentiment to the gothic marvelous, from one polarity of mid-century criticism to another, as though seeking within the general boundaries of mid-century revaluations the terms of his own poetry. Nowhere in the second half-century do the opposing values appear more sharply drawn than in Johnson's reaction to Gray. The last great spokesman of Augustan humanism confronted, with almost unmitigated severity, the only major poet of the mid-century revolution. It is a division more sharply and clearly visible than anything of its kind in the entire age.

To look back upon both Collins and Gray is to recognize the frustration of greatness on a major scale. There is little doubt that each promised more than he performed. The reasons are not to be found in the brevity of Collins's productive years or in Gray's presumed isolation. Rather, the reasons are located in a mid-century poetic of such drastic limitations that it offered to the poet no specifically contemporary act of mind and no imitative models other than the extrapolated sublimities of past poets. It was not a fertile field; it offered little to its best poets who found what little there was, and who more often than not found in the marvels of an animated sensibility mere shadows of the mind.

It can only be anticlimactic to consider the poetry of Joseph and Thomas Warton, though each deserves something more than perfunctory acknowledgment. They are so central to the mid-century revolution that it is hardly imaginable without them. Yet their scholarship today is known only to antiquarians; their poetry lacks even the decent burial of a modern edition. Each wrote the poem by which he is best remembered at an early age and neither wrote another of comparable reputation. Their poetic careers, if that is quite the right term, were decidedly ancillary to their other interests.[47]

However, "The Pleasures of Melancholy" remains the best example of the Miltonic *penseroso* moodiness at mid-century. In that poem the landscape vibrates with atmospheric effects: night is "tempestuous," winds "howling," rain "beating," hail "drifting," the vault of heaven "spangled," and more, much more, of the same. Contemplation is the "Mother of musings," the "queen sublime," leading to "solemn glooms / Congenial with my soul." Thomas Warton moves restlessly through the landscape: "Beneath yon ruin'd abbey's moss-grown piles / Oft let me sit." Somewhat later he "tread[s]," then "pace[s]," subsequently "watch[es]" and later witnesses the "ghostly shape" inviting "with beck'ning hand." The hour is initially twilight, the "pale moon / Pours her long-levell'd rule of streaming light"; the caverns are "dark"; the "world / Is clad in Midnight's raven-colour'd robe"; the "flame / Of taper dim" sheds "a livid glare" along "the glimm'ring walls."

Nothing could be more theatrical, more stage-managed, the setting for a drama in which the only actors are Warton, Melancholy, Midnight, the "ghostly shape," and the "sacred Genius of the night." As the dim candle burns, Warton's soul is wrapped in "religious horror." It is all splendidly chilling, graveyard, gothic, and adolescent (as was Warton when he wrote it). Melancholy and her attendants provide the appropriate context for visionary experience, for those "mystic visions" such "as Spenser saw . . . or Milton knew." Wrapped in self-enchantments, Warton prepares for visions of "Fancy's magic maze," for Milton's "abstracted thought," for sights of "Seraphim / . . . tow'ring arm'd in adamant and gold." It is excessively jeweled but not without affinities to Gray's legion of personifications or the "gentlest influence" of Collins's "Ode to Evening." Its characteristics persist into Wordsworth's poetry: "the poet being stirred initially by the natural aspects of an object such as a quiet evening, and then, as the silence increases and the poem progresses, he has a glimpse into the incorporeal and finds there, not just genial human qualities, but the mighty Being and a 'sound like thunder—everlastingly.'"[48]

For the young Warton visionary experience existed subliminally, the passions derived from the context—wooed from it—were transmuted into poetic realities, into visions of what was grand or sublime. It was a curious basis on which to write poetry, but from a pleasing horror arose the visionary ideal hidden within it, and the enchantment of the imagination, over which the goddess Contemplation presides, is the true subject of the poem. As Warton descends into the buried life within, a descent for which "stealing sleep" bathing him "in opiate dews" suggests a distinction between what is available to conscious and unconscious mind, the visions of old are courted by the reverential recreation of a summoning context. The "sacred Genius of the night" is the poetic genius of all that is not normally available to the ordinary identity of the poet: the sacred genius is the raptured poet of the night within.

Abraham Tucker provided the associational justification for Warton's procedure in the poem. Tucker suggested a distinction between conscious and unconscious: the uncon-

scious is a repository of "ideas" no longer available to the
mind upon demand, but capable of being evoked by certain
stimuli. The mind, said Tucker, "does not call up all our
thoughts directly by its own immediate command, but seizes
on some clue whereby it draws in all the rest."[49] The conception that art animates and intensifies the powers of mind had
long been a vital part of associational theory. In the "Pleasures," Warton suggested the process by which that intensification might be communicated to the reader through the
work of art and, not incidentally, recreated the like process
experienced by the visionary poet. As Archibald Alison was
to propose in 1790: "It is then, indeed, in this powerless state
of reverie, when we are carried on by our conceptions, not
guiding them, that the deepest emotions of beauty or sublimity are felt."[50] The relaxation of the reason and will as a
condition for certain kinds of experience otherwise unavailable has a long and honorable history in English poetry. For
our purposes it is easily traced back to "Il Penseroso" and
forward to characteristic states of mind found in Wordsworth's and Keats's poetry. The deliberate invocation of
self-hypnotic moods as experientially transformative suggests another exploration of the marvelous that lies deep
within human nature. The terms of Warton's progression:
"oblivion," "silence," "sleep," "solitude," "dreams," point to
the obligatory conditions of recovery.

While "The Pleasures of Melancholy" is Warton's best-
known poem, his most characteristic works invoked the remote British past, not only in such odes as "The Crusade" or
"The Grave of King Arthur," both published in 1777, but
also in several of the New Year odes and odes celebratory of
George III's birthday after Warton became poet laureate in
1785. He was, as might be expected, most at home within the
ambience of Arthurian or late medieval England, and it was
seldom long before, as in "Written at Vale-Royal Abbey in

Cheshire," "Gothic portraiture," "taper'd rites," and "vision-ary gleams" of the "tranced mind" make their appearance. Johnson must have been annoyed to read "honied flowers" in one of Warton's odes, but, like Collins and Gray, Warton enjoyed the antiquarian flavoring, and such phrases as "thymy mound," "sedgy shore," and "prickly thistle" abound.

Invariably one of his odes was written to Upton on his edition of the *Faerie Queene,* and in the piece celebrating George's marriage to Charlotte in 1761 Warton could not resist comparing her to Spenser's Elizabeth. The ode "Sent to a Friend, on his leaving a favourite Village in Hampshire" was written to Joseph on the occasion of his brother's departure for abroad. Who now, asks Thomas, shall take observant notice of rural scenes? The question leads into the pretty conceit that Joseph's absence will demythologize nature:

> No pearl-crown'd Maids, with wily look,
> Rise beckoning from the reedy brook.
> Around the glow-worm's glimmering bank,
> No Fairies run in fiery rank;
> Nor brush, half-seen, in airy tread,
> The violet's unprinted head.   (ll. 63–68)

Fancy withdraws her offspring, and, as Thomas's poem concludes, "a bare heath's unfruitful plain / Usurp'd the wisard's proud domain."

The sonnets, of which Warton wrote nine, or somewhat less than half the number of his odes, reveal the same interests adapted to the shorter form. "To Mr. Gray" pays the debt of "gratitude" to "The Bard" for "many a raptur'd thought and vision wild." Others, such as "Written in a Blank Leaf of Dugdale's Monasticon," "Written at Stonehenge," and "On King Arthur's Round Table at Winchester," rehearse the familiar themes of Warton's poetry, and we are often invited to "muse on many an ancient tale renown'd." It is almost uncharitable to speak slightingly of Warton's poetry; he did so unabashedly relish the fairy land of British antiquity that his whole life, both as scholar and poet, was an attempt to recreate it for his own time. Who would guess, if he did not know, that the man of heavy respectability looking out at us from Reynolds's portrait was in love with a fairy vision of the marvelous?

When in 1750 Thomas wrote his ode "Sent to a Friend," he was apparently remembering Joseph's "The Enthusiast: or the Lover of Nature," written in 1740. It is the ideal companion poem for "The Pleasures of Melancholy." Thomas was perhaps more conspicuously literary in his references to Spenser and to Milton, to Shakespeare and to Otway, but Joseph noticed the superiority of Shakespeare's "warblings wild" to "the lays of artful Addison, / Coldly correct." "The Pleasures of Melancholy" more insistently courted the gothic mood, whereas "The Enthusiast" expressed rapture in the simple, uncorrupted pleasures of nature. The "Ode to Fancy," included in the 1746 edition of Joseph's poems, is very much in the same mode. It may owe something in particular to Dryden's "Alexander's Feast," and Warton's Fancy performs a function analogous to Dryden's power of music. Like music, Fancy is the instrumental agent of various passions, and as Timotheus leads Alexander through the militant emotions to the melting passion of love, so too does Fancy conduct the varied tones of Warton's song. Fancy, "queen of numbers," is to

> Animate some chosen swain,
> Who, fill'd with unexhausted fire,
> May boldly smite the sounding lyre,
> Who with some new unequall'd song,
> May rise above the rhyming throng,
> O'er all our list'ning passions reign,
> O'erwhelm our souls with joy and pain,
> With terrour shake, and pity move,
> Rouse with revenge, or melt with love.

The relation between poetry and music was not an un-common topic of English criticism in the middle and later years of the century. Charles Avison in 1753 had popularized the term *expression* defining it as "the power of exciting all the most agreeable passions of the soul." Ten years later John Brown suggested that music was the natural incantation of passion. The musicality of untutored genius ("woodnotes wild") informs the lyric of primitive grace, serving as a vehicle for the *expressive* and *suggestive*. Burke was to claim in 1757 that poetry moves the passions by "conveying the *affections* of the mind from one to another." And Sir William Jones in 1772 remarked that "the finest parts of poetry, music, and painting, are expressive of the passions, and operate on our minds by sympathy."[51]

Inevitably such criteria focused attention on the poet himself. Collins wrote on the poetical character, the speaker of the "Elegy" is himself a poet, as is the persona of "The Enthusiast." The Romantics did not invent this persona; he was the product especially of mid-century self-consciousness. The more that poetry became the expression of emotions, the more the poet moved toward the center of attention as someone possessed, above other and ordinary men, of an exquisite capacity to feel and to express universal emotions. The poet was therefore justified by these writers in the only way available to them. The poet is a man of sensibility; from sensibility he derives the power to bring into being visions unrealized by other men. He is a conjurer of lost realities and in the Wartonian poems more often than not a magician or illusionist. The conception is consistent with the mid-century critical revaluations, and the poet as high priest of feeling is the creation of writers who cannot otherwise use the past. "The Enthusiast" itself is a title borrowed from Shaftesbury, enforcing the idea of enthusiasm as the prerogative of genius.

Joseph Warton's other poems are generally inferior to

those of his brother, and while his diction is less deliberately archaic and the use of British history far less important, gothic moods are evident in the odes "To Superstition" and "To Solitude." Two of his poems, the "Ode to Evening" and the "Ode to Liberty," bear the same titles as poems in Collins's collection. Warton's range is anything but various, though "The Dying Indian" reads like a set piece from one of Dryden's heroic tragedies and half of the short poem "The Revenge of America" is composed of a speech by a Peruvian king enraged by the woes that Spanish lust for gold has brought upon his country.

Like Collins and Gray, but with far less success, the Wartons commonly wrote short poems offering little sustained exploration of theme and no widening context of values created by their poetic representation of the passions. Again, it was no wonder. To regard Spenser, Shakespeare, and Milton as "copious magazines" of the "most lively painting" was productive of a poetry in which the bold and striking image was the sine qua non of literary aspiration. The poetry of passion was fast culminating in a literature revelatory of the limits of passion conceived as a fit and entire subject for poetry. Expressive undoubtedly of a yearning for the ideal, it almost entirely failed to communicate a sense of the relation between ideal and ordinary experience.

Of James Macpherson even less needs to be said. He is, like Chatterton, a historical curiosity, a purveyor of historical fictions. His vogue was, and has remained, an oddity of a particular historical moment, and by no account can he be enlisted in the ranks of important British poets. He added nothing substantially new to the poetic values of mid-century, though he found a means for giving expression to them in accord with the fashion for cultural primitivism. The poetry of passion, to which Macpherson contributed, represented the attempt to impose a pattern on reality derived from man's genuine perceptions of his human nature, a nature verified historically but unilluminated by the possibilities of transcendence. Thus, Gray may at moments seem a Wordsworthian manqué; thus, for Blake (as we shall see) Gray was an undeclared Blakean, a prophet who needed only to have his true intentions elucidated by a sympathetic and knowing interpreter. First and foremost the revolution of mid-century was a full-scale attempt to reveal the essentials of man's life in time devoid of Platonic idealism or Christian humanism, a world in which the verities of the human spirit were seen, ultimately, as secular and finite.

The passions themselves, the recreated subject of the poetic marvelous, were the legacy bequeathed by the mid-century poets to their Romantic successors. Passion was to be transformed and reoriented by Blake and Wordsworth, put into relation with a reconstructed image of human nature derived from the ordinary and probable events of human life. Another poetic revolution of greater magnitude was about to come forth, not by entirely obviating the achievement of mid-century but by altering and transmuting much that those poets had left behind. The mid-century poets and critics had turned from the cultivated garden of English Augustanism to the luxuriant overgrowth of sensibility. To their successors they left much that was newly fertile, but of the further uses to which it could be put they offered few clues. They had in fact left their household gods behind, and it remained for the next generation to reestablish the familiar touchstones of Christian supernaturalism by resettling them in the new context of the passions.

4
William Blake

Blake's relation to his mid-century predecessors has been impressively defined for us. "He belongs," says Northrop Frye, "neither to the Augustans nor to the Romantics, either as a representative or a rebel. He belongs to another age altogether; the age, in poetry, of Collins, Percy, Gray, Cowper, Smart, Chatterton, Burns, Ossian and the Wartons. Blake's masters in poetry were Gray, Collins, Chatterton and Ossian." But were they? It is a position to be challenged. The premises on which Frye's assumption rests are misleading, premises which may be presented very briefly: "the poets of the age of Blake wanted to go back to mythopoeic poetry."[1]

Not exactly. They did not want to make myth, indeed did not know what making myth required or involved. They wanted instead the direct and immediate apprehension of the human sensibility, and they invested their own powers in summoning those passions in which, to them, the ideal reposed. The orientations of such poets only superficially resemble Blake's, and the transformation to which he subjected whatever influences he derived from them is the most striking fact of his relation to his predecessors.

Blake profusely illustrated English poetry, as well as the *Book of Job* and the *Divine Comedy*. He illustrated most of Milton's major poetry, Young's *Night Thoughts*, Blair's *The Grave*, scenes from Shakespeare, Bunyan's *Pilgrim's Progress*, and much from both the Old and New Testaments. Particularly to the point here, he prepared 116 engravings to Gray's poems. Available information suggests that the work was started around 1794 and completed by 1805 at the latest. It provides a unique example of interpretive criticism offered by one poet on another. As Irene Tayler observes, Blake's illustrations expose "the real vision half-dormant in the language of Gray's poems,"[2] but, as Tayler fully recognizes, they are more than merely this. The illustrations are not always in accord with Gray's intentions, but powerfully suggest the terms in which Blake preferred to read the poems. He saw in Gray's poems a text other readers have never quite discovered, but one wholly related to Blake's own progress as a poet. In his treatment of them, Gray's poems assume more energy of perception than we normally grant them, and this is achieved by Blake through a selection and emphasis of detail often built upon the merest hints that Gray provided. It is fair to say that Blake reenvisioned Gray's poems; his illustrations are not simply visual explanations but reinterpretations and reorganizations of the latent potentialities of vision which Blake discerned within them. In this sense the illustrations are reconstructions, using the materials of Gray's own perceptions to discover the Blakean visions lurking within them.

In the eighth of ten illustrations to the "Ode on a Distant Prospect of Eton College," Blake illustrated lines 81 to 96, beginning

> Lo, in the vale of years beneath
> A grisly troop are seen,
> The painful family of Death,
> More hideous than their Queen.

Tayler describes the design and then remarks: "The point is clear: the man who grows old in helpless fear of himself and fear for his future, who submits himself to the blinding restrictions of a Urizenic existence, will finally become what he fears and succumb to the god he has created." Nothing could be further from Gray's intentions; he would not only have been astonished by such a rendering but would have found it entirely antithetical to his purposes. To the same point John Grant notes also that in the fourth illustration for Gray's "Ode to Adversity," "the harsh figure of Adversity holds a scribal figure in her lap. Gray thinks this is good tutelage, but Blake shows by the compasses she holds that she is fit only to teach law and order to 'Virtue,' not the truth that makes us free."[3]

Such examples of Blake's criticism and reconstruction of Gray's poems could be multiplied indefinitely from the designs. Much the same commentary as offered by Tayler and Grant has been put forward in relation to Blake's poetic use of Ossian. Kathleen Raine notices the Ossianic diction in the *Poetical Sketches* and particularly in *Thel,* whose heroine, as Raine comments, "has all the external attributes of the Ossianic heroines." But "beneath that surface of Ossianic imagery Thel, Leutha, and Oothoon have hard symbolic bones never to be found in their prototypes, Vinvela, Malvina, Oithona, and the rest of Macpherson's gentle mournful ghosts."[4]

Yet more than a cautionary note is required. Much more nearly related to the poetry of Blake, and to Wordsworth, is the tradition of the religious sublime poem in the eighteenth century. The middle and later years of the century do not offer many examples of first-rate religious poetry, but Young's *Night Thoughts* began to appear in 1742, Smart's "A Song to David" in 1763 (*Jubilate Agno* was begun in 1759 but not published until the twentieth century), and Cowper's *The Task* in 1785. Within the century the divine poem has a long history, going back at least to Pope's *Messiah* and drawing strength and critical support from Dennis and Addison in the early years and from Lowth in the middle years.

It is a mode in which, with very few exceptions, much of the least interesting poetry of the period was written and little of the very best. Yet its historical importance is far in excess of the quality of the poetry produced. Between Milton and Blake the possibilities for a poetry of Christian super-naturalism were kept alive largely by writers to whom I have referred, and through them the poetry of the religious sub-lime maintained its hold on the eighteenth-century imagina-tion. For many writers of the century, from Dennis to Johnson, only the religious sublime poem could plausibly combine the disparate values of the probable and the marvel-ous, and Johnson most tellingly made the point: "Of the *probable* and the *marvellous,* two parts of a vulgar epic poem which immerge the critic in deep consideration, the *Paradise Lost* requires little to be said. It contains the history of a miracle, of Creation and Redemption; it displays the power and the mercy of the Supreme Being; the probable therefore is marvellous, and the marvellous is probable."[5]

Of the writers in the middle years, Smart is perhaps the most important of those who sustained this tradition, but he is also very different from such poets as Thomson and Young, who sought the evidence for God in nature. As David Morris says, Smart "is not primarily interested in discovering evidence of God's design; he seeks, instead, signs of his exis-tence, aspects of his Being, participation in his inexplicable ongoing processes."[6] Blake, however, derived the necessity for his principal theme, innocence and experience, from Mil-ton's theological "errors" in *Paradise Lost.* As with many writers of the religious sublime poem in the eighteenth cen-tury, Smart is not properly to be numbered among Blake's masters.[7] It is far more reliable, in relation to the tradition of the religious sublime poem, to depend less upon occasions of specific influence manifest in Blake's poems than upon a con-tinuing Christian dedication that invariably links Blake, however oddly at times, with his predecessors. What is in-volved is the transmutation of a tradition, commonly characterizing a complex relationship under the heading of *influence,* and Blake's orientation differs as substantially and as radically from that of Young or Smart as, for example, Wordsworth's does from Cowper's.

Frye's indiscriminate grouping of mid-century poets suggests a confusion of traditions, a confusion that obscures the various employment of Milton by mid-century poets. What Collins, Gray, and the Wartons required from Milton was very different from what Thomson, Young, Smart, and Cowper derived. Some overlappings exist, but whereas the former writers may be associated with the rhetorical sublime—as Milton's shorter poems offered justification for a secular sublimity of the passions—the latter writers may more profitably be viewed in relation to *Paradise Lost.* It is at least arguable that the early lyric poetry of both Blake and Wordsworth suggests a confluence of the lyric poem and the religious sublime, the adaptation of the latter to the requirements of the former. The lyric offered both Blake and Wordsworth a vehicle for the dramatic characterization of human nature contending with the contraries of innocence and experience.

It is worth noticing further that the poetry of the religious sublime was written largely by poets outside the influence of the Wartons and their circle. While Joseph Warton dedicated the first volume of his *Essay on Pope* to Edward Young, Gray's friend Mason, intent on amusing him with an insight into the taste of one of his German acquaintances, noted that Young was her favorite author. Smart was treated not much better by Mason: "I have seen his Song to David & from thence conclude him as mad as ever." Gray, writing much earlier to Wharton on the subject of Akenside's *Pleasures of the Imagination,* readily dismissed it as "often obscure & even unintelligible, & too much infected with the Hutchinson-Jargon."[8]

Thus, Blake's return to the mid-century romancers does not define the continuity of what is vital to mid-eighteenth-century poetry any more than the return of Collins, Gray, and the Wartons to the great poets of the English tradition, to Spenser, Shakespeare, and Milton, offers evidence of a continuing poetic tradition. Blake's task, and Wordsworth's, was the large-scale reconstructive one of creating another idea of human nature to displace the merely *romantic* image that was the legacy of mid-century poetry. The work of the three decades 1740 to 1770 had been deliberately reactionary in spirit. The work of the years 1789 to 1807 was to result in the displacement of the mid-century heritage, and in this regard the beginnings of Romanticism constituted the second major exploration of the probable and the marvelous in the eighteenth century.

That the exploration was occasioned by a reaction to post-Augustan poetry is not to say that there was little to be derived from it by the new poets. Abbie Findlay Potts has well demonstrated Wordsworth's debt to the eighteenth century, and much the same job, though within a larger frame of reference, has been accomplished for Blake by Kathleen Raine.[9] The point is, however, that Blake and Wordsworth began anew, much as Collins and Gray did a generation earlier. In doing so they maintained as a fundamental mark of reference the entire protracted concern with the probable and marvelous that had remained, as I have suggested, the central topic of literary criticism. When Blake and Wordsworth grew into poetic maturity in the last decade of the eighteenth century, nothing less important than the justification of the cultural centrality of poetry was the task they set themselves, nothing less critical than the marvelous of the human mind was the subject they resumed.

It is unfortunate that Blake has been viewed as an especially difficult poet, abstruse and obscure, for the obvious importance of the *Songs of Innocence* resides in its attempt to state the immanent divinity of man in terms of the unfallen imagination and to provide a basis for the reconstructed image of human nature. Yet his poetry has been commonly regarded as highly problematical, so much so that it has led at least one modern scholar to complain of the "substitution of exegesis for criticism which characterises the bulk of critical writing about the work of William Blake."[10] Blake therefore has become the kind of poet who inspires critics to offer techniques for the reading of his poems. E. D. Hirsch has suggested that the "'dialectical' meaning of the *Songs of Innocence* . . . exists within the poems themselves; that is why they have their fullest impact when they are properly read—seriatim and as an autonomous whole." In the same vein Robert Gleckner has proposed the necessity to be mindful of symbol and context in the *Songs:* "many of Blake's symbols are recurrent, so that once a symbol's basic significance is revealed in a kind of archetypal context, each successive context adds association to association within the song series."[11] Both Hirsch and Gleckner are fine critics, but both suggestions are wrong and unfortunately misleading; there is in fact no method, either dialectical or archetypal, for the reading of Blake's *Songs of Innocence.* I do not mean to imply by this statement that the *Songs* cannot be read but that there are ways in which they should not be read. Some assumptions need to be put aside.

The first of these is that the songs of *Innocence* are exclusively about the state of innocence. They are not always so and sometimes very importantly not so. Occasionally the songs are about the state of experience. It seems also true that the *Songs of Innocence* is an exploratory volume; that is, composed of poems in which Blake unmethodically explored the state of innocence as he was coming to conceive of it between the years 1784 and 1789. Therefore it is not always easy and not always desirable to find explicit relationships among all the songs. There is good evidence for remaining highly doubtful about any particular order in which *Innocence* is to be found. From 1789 to the last years of Blake's life and through five different editions he continued to change the order of the songs. As David Erdman points out: "In no two copies of *Innocence* . . . are the plates containing the songs arranged in exactly the same order." These are the obvious difficulties confronting any "seriatim" reading of the *Songs*. While Hirsch resists the tendency to systematize *Innocence,* he nevertheless commits himself to the view that "man's sacramental re-enactment of Christ's care for man is one of the two principal themes of the *Songs of Innocence.*" Because of this burden of consistency, Hirsch argues that the narrator of "The Chimney Sweeper" of *Innocence* "plays the part of guardian to little Tom Dacre." Consequently, Hirsch reads the last line of the poem—"So if all do their duty, they need not fear harm"—as a "misfortune" which "jars in the poem."[12]

So, too, does Martin Nurmi propose that "doing one's duty here means primarily going up chimneys without having to be forced, and the 'harm' is the very real punishment given boys who would not climb." Both critics reveal a degree of desperation before the shifting perspectives of Blake's songs, a shifting perspective that is not solved by Gleckner's proposal of an accretively established symbolic context. Thus of the beadles' wands in "Holy Thursday" Gleckner remarks: "The wand is 'white as snow' to suggest the frigidity of man-made moral purity as opposed to the warmth of young, energetic, exuberant innocence."[13] Gleckner is undoubtedly right, but presumably white is a symbol in "Holy Thursday" even as "red & blue & green" are symbols of the flower children of innocence. Therefore if we know what *white* means in one context, we will know what it means in another as "each successive context adds association to association within the song series." But Tom Dacre's hair before it was shaved was white, and the little English boy who will come to love the little black boy is white. In no way are these three uses of the word *white* interchangeable, and in only two of the three instances can the word be construed as having a symbolic function at all. †The songs do not work in the way Gleckner suggests because point of view is qualified by the perspective of the speaker of each song, and innocence is seen variously by various speakers. One might go so far as to remark that each of Blake's speakers is himself (or herself) in a different relation to innocence, and not all are either within innocence or sympathetic to it. As everything we know about the composition of the *Songs* indicates, between 1784 and 1789 Blake was exploring various relations to innocence within the large-scale context he was unmethodically constructing.

Yet, at the same time, one must attempt definitions—not merely readings of the individual poems but a conception of what the songs are about. The most immediate form of innocence is that state of complete containment and contentment within a joyfully animated nature in which human and divine, animal and vegetable, are correspondent parts of an undivided vision. But such a definition is emphatically not pertinent to all the actors within *Innocence*. Hirsch's view that the last line of "The Chimney Sweeper" is a "misfortune" is itself unfortunate, since it is apparent that the speaker of the poem is himself unhappily corrupted and therefore speaks from the perspective that experience necessarily takes upon innocence. The autobiographical data of the first stanza is not a gratuity in the poem:

> When my mother died I was very young,
> And my father sold me while yet my tongue,
> Could scarcely cry weep weep weep weep,
> So your chimneys I sweep & in soot I sleep.

Rather, such information supplies us with what we must know of the speaker. The guardian mother of innocence has died; the cruel father has sold him into slavery. It is inevitable therefore that he speaks with the rationalizing voice of experience—"Hush Tom never mind it, for when your head's bare, / You know that the soot cannot spoil your white hair"—and offers the hypocritical moral enforcing the idea of "duty" at the end of the poem. Tom's vision, however, has nothing to do with duty; it has everything to do with the vision of innocence that lives within the child, which sustains itself if only one is faithful to its own terms.

The apparent companion poem to "The Chimney Sweeper" is "Holy Thursday" of *Innocence*. Like the speaker of the first poem, the speaker of "Holy Thursday" preaches the moral of his own corrupted vision in which "pity" is the rigorous and stony-eyed truth of an abstract morality. In both poems the speakers are in effect the real victims of the morality they acknowledge, as the children of "Holy Thursday" cannot be and as Tom Dacre obviously is not. In relation to both poems, one must read "The Divine Image" as setting out imagistically the true conditions of compassion. "The Divine Image" is not founded on an abstract morality, but it is clearly located in those human virtues which are, finally, "virtues of delight."

It is almost axiomatic in the *Songs of Innocence* that any specific divorce between morality and the human image is suspect, as any separation between human and divine is suspect, as any alienation of human from animal life is equally suspect. There cannot be an image which is too anthropomorphic in the *Songs of Innocence* because an innocent world is an extension of the child; the father in heaven is not a remote deity, but the child's imagined form of the adult as, for that matter, the lamb is the imagined form of Christ who "became a little child." Earth is beneficent because to the child it is the incarnate form of God, as the creatures are the separate and collective manifestations of that God. Thus Harold Bloom's suggestion that the "human child of *Songs of Innocence* is a changeling, reared by a foster nurse who cannot recognize his divinity, and whose ministrations entrap him in a universe of death" cannot be more in error. To make the statement is to read the *Songs of Innocence* from the perspective of "The Mental Traveller," but not from those perspectives which the songs themselves provide on their context. Bloom remarks on "The Divine Image" that "until its matching contrary comes to it in *Songs of Experience,* the poem's prime characteristic is its deliberate incompleteness."[14] There is, however, nothing incomplete about "The Divine Image" within the context of the *Songs of Innocence;* because of its presence one understands the false witness borne by the speakers of "The Chimney Sweeper" and "Holy Thursday." The presence within the collection of "The Divine Image" steadies our comprehension of the songs and lends surety to our readings of other poems within *Innocence.* The important point to bear in mind about the *Songs of Innocence* is that innocence is always innocent, but not all the figures in *Innocence* are innocent.

The poems vary widely from the immediate conditions of the protective and protected world, in which immanent delight is the wholly governing virtue of that world, to such a poem as "The Little Black Boy," in which the mother's understanding is qualified and defeated by the child's invulnerable innocence. Poems of the first sort, however, would include "Spring," "Laughing Song," and "Infant Joy," all characterized by the pervasiveness of an unreflective delight, an immediate apprehension of song or laughter or joy as the primary principle of life in the world. But this condition is not always sustained in the songs if only because the character of the speaker changes from poem to poem. "A Cradle Song" and "A Dream" are both songs about innocence, but they are spoken by speakers not themselves within the context of innocence. In both poems a pitying protective figure mourns the imminence of experience, but, like the nurse of the "Nurse's Song" or the speaker of "The Ecchoing Green," can do nothing about the inevitable oncoming of experience which only he or she perceives. Such poems are prophetic of experience, aware, that is, of the lengthening shadows cast over the garden. The perspective of the speaker communicates the fact that the tenure of innocence is indefinite, that as a state of the soul it is subject to time and circumstance and therefore perishable.

While the fall from innocence is inevitable, there is also evidence that even as early as 1784–1789 Blake recognized such a fall as desirable. There is for one thing the evidence of the two poems, "The Little Girl Lost" and "The Little Girl Found" (later transferred to *Experience*), in which Lyca willingly submits to the descent into experience, a descent largely realized imagistically through the implicit sexual encounter that governs her submission. There is also the evidence of *Thel,* composed at approximately the same time, in which protracted innocence results in the rationalizing morality apparent in Thel's motto.

But the earliest versions of the *Songs of Innocence* suggest a wide-ranging conception of innocence, from the child's complete identity with the natural and created world to the willing farewell to innocence of the Lyca poems. In between there are such important poems as "The Chimney Sweeper," "Holy Thursday," "The Divine Image," and "The Little Black Boy." Bloom says that the last is "the best poem in the series."[15] It is surely one of the more interesting in that the protective guardian figure of the mother is troubled by the necessity to account for the difference between black and white skins. In order to do so she develops, inadvertently perhaps, a myth of the Fall based on the conception of Original Sin and the complementary myth of Redemption based on trial and endurance. To this myth the child, speaking the poem in his own voice (an important consideration), adds his own role as protective guardian of the little white boy. The drama of protected innocence is reenacted by the little black boy who in effect will bear for the little white boy the burden of love that his mother now bears for him.

It is customary to criticize the mother's "confusion" in the poem, but we should remember that she is explaining the occasion of blackness to her son as evidence of the trial that God's love imposes upon us. Those with black bodies have absorbed more of God's love than have those with white bodies. At the least it is a very sweet maternal notion. Bloom states that the child's "urge to work out the consequences of such truth reveals the inadequacy of Innocence, of the natural context to sustain any idealizations whatsoever."[16] However, because the child accepts his mother's teaching as truth, he works out an analogy between the truth which pertains on the level of nature and that which pertains on the level of the divine. The little black boy experiences no sundering of the natural and divine; what is true on one level is true on another. Nothing could be closer to that state of the soul which *Innocence* celebrates than such a mode of reasoning.

While there are some songs of *Innocence* in which the end of innocence is clearly suggested, there are no poems that reflect the inadequacy of innocence, none that reflect merely a sentimental and hence ironic conception of innocence. Even "Night," the poem most susceptible to such interpretation, does not deny the protective guardianship of the angels. Nor is this protective guardianship qualified in any sense by the speaking voice of the poem. Eternity ("immortal day") implies the restoration of innocence. "Night," as the title implies, has for its immediate context the state of experience, but it is at least arguable that "Night," unlike "The Little Girl Lost" and "The Little Girl Found," does not present experience as a desirable progression of the soul from one state to another. On the contrary, the lion of the poem is not the symbolically purgative figure of Blake's tiger of *Experience* but the predator who yearns to be released from his wrathful nature and delivered to the mild conditions of the peaceable kingdom.

Of all the songs initially placed by Blake within *Innocence* only "The Little Girl Lost" and "The Little Girl Found" insist upon the value of the transition from innocence to experience. It is conjectural, but attractive to believe, that Blake came in time to perceive the full implications of a contrary state of the soul, implications which are, however, only occasionally apparent in the earliest versions of the *Songs of Innocence*. It is only therefore from the standpoint of experience that one can talk, as Gleckner does, about the "tragedy" of innocence.[17] By definition there can be no tragedy in innocence, and not until Blake composed *Thel* did he perceive clearly that protracted innocence is itself a tragedy.

The poem that most effectively leads the reader from *Innocence* to *Experience* is "On Another's Sorrow," usually printed at the end of the *Songs* and perhaps standing as a conclusion to it. Here, if anywhere in *Innocence,* the affinity of grief for grief suggests an end to innocence. But by the time we have come to "On Another's Sorrow," we have run an extraordinary gamut of possibilities pertinent to innocence, and the state of innocence has been explored from a number of different perspectives. Though none of these effectively challenge that state, some of them communicate how innocence appears from the perspective of experience ("The Chimney Sweeper" and "Holy Thursday"). At least one song dramatizes the invulnerability of innocence confronted by the facts of experience ("The Little Black Boy"). At least

two represent the impending end of innocence ("The Ecchoing Green" and "Nurse's Song"). Four show the restoration of innocence before the imminent and threatening
conditions of experience ("The Little Boy Lost" and "The
Little Boy Found," "Night," and "A Dream"). Several make
apparent the quality of immanent delight that lies at the heart
of innocence ("Laughing Song," "Spring," and "Infant Joy"),
and some simply reinforce the image of true guardianship
through the protective figures of mother or shepherd or vegetable life ("The Shepherd," "A Cradle Song," "The Blos-
som," and probably "The Divine Image"). That Blake
should have transferred "The Little Girl Lost" and "The Little Girl Found," "The Voice of the Ancient Bard," and "The
School Boy" from *Innocence* to *Experience* makes perfect
sense in the light of the argument I have been presenting. In
one way or another (definitely not in the same way), the four
transferred poems are songs of experience. Because of the
diversity of the *Songs of Innocence,* however, no single ordering principle prevails.

Songs of Innocence is not a long poem; it is a composition of
short, experimental lyrics that has no seriatim unity, no accretively established context of symbols, no dialectical relationship among its parts. The direct background for these poems
is that of an even more eclectic assortment, the *Poetical
Sketches* of 1783, in which one can dimly perceive the early
and incipient awareness of both states of the soul developing
in Blake's poetry. The song beginning "I love the jocund
dance" is a very early version of "The Ecchoing Green,"
whereas "Mad Song" and the two songs, one beginning
"Memory, hither come," and the other, "How sweet I
roam'd from field to field," are early songs of experience.

But if there is no method as such for reading the *Songs of
Innocence,* there are in any event values that remain relatively
stable within *Innocence.* These may be listed as follows: (1)

delight is a state of the soul entirely consonant with innocence and never rendered ironically; (2) abstract moral propositions are suspect, and the one who voices them speaks from within the context of experience; (3) no two poems have the same speaker or employ identical perspectives on the state of innocence; (4) if we exclude the four songs later transferred to *Experience,* the state of experience is never viewed as advantageous; (5) the maternal guardian is always good, if not always an effective guardian; (6) the paternal guardian is always bad unless specifically associated with God the father; (7) all animal and vegetable life is good. With these seven propositions we can find our way through the songs of *Innocence* recognizing them for what they are: an early assortment of poems variously stating the terms of innocence and organized nonprogressively, nonassociatively, nonlogically. There is no ruling principle of organization—a fact that may explain why Blake could not rest satisfied with any of his various editions. For that matter, there is no fidelity to the conception of the songs as "happy" as stated in the "Introduction."

Yet the achievement of *Innocence* resides in the creation of a newly marvelous world of immanent divinity. The *Songs* are not in the manner of Smart's *Hymns for the Amusement of Children.* Rather, Blake's *Songs* insist upon the fact that perception is a function of the imagination, or, in such poems as "The Chimney Sweeper" and "Holy Thursday," a consequence of the deformity and corruption of the imagination. In this regard the songs are not instructional exercises but dramatizations of the mental states which determine vision. As does Wordsworth, Blake begins with character. His speakers enact their perceptions, which means simply that what and how they see is demonstrative of who and what they are—vision is their fate. The speakers of "The Chimney Sweeper" and "Holy Thursday" believe they have applied good moral teaching and that in so doing they are honoring God and man. Blake lets us know that they are merely victims of the morality they promulgate, that "duty" and "pity" are the ministers of Urizenic bondage, a state of mind from which arises the fear of human energy and human passion that will come to characterize the state of experience.

• Of the songs that Blake subsequently transferred to *Experience,* "The Little Girl Lost" and "The Little Girl Found" are the most useful for suggesting immediately his growing conception of the relation between the states of innocence and experience. Both "Little Girl" poems are the direct counterparts of *Thel,* and Lyca's resolution, achieved in the first of the companion poems, is the opposite of Thel's. Where she flees from the recognition of her own morality and returns to the land of protracted innocence, presided over by the senile figures of Har and Heva, Lyca willingly courts the descent into experience and seeks through sleep (Blake's metaphor here for the fall from one state to another) an encounter with knowledge inimical to the conditions of innocence. The beasts of prey that visit the sleeping girl are more than generally ambiguous terrors; they are, rather, the evocations of passions compatible with the frowning night and with the assumption of maturity and knowledge required by the state of experience. More specifically the passions suggest sexual knowledge, tempered in context by the pity of the kingly lion, the Christlike and regal beast whose compassion for Lyca is manifest even while the "sleeping maid" is conveyed to caves.

Lyca is disrobed to suggest vulnerability to awakening sexual desire. The situation is not unlike Oothoon's in the *Visions of the Daughters of Albion.* Less obviously Lyca's nakedness implies the casting off of old forms prior to the assumption of new ones. The pity of the lion who weeps "ruby tears" from "eyes of flame" is the manifestation of

Christ's love for Lyca, whose submission to the terrors and griefs of experience is nothing less than an acceptance of her entire human nature. For Blake, as for Milton, the Fall is a painful fact of the human condition; but unlike Milton, Blake sees it not as the result of a specific act of disobedience, and therefore punitive, but a necessary state for growth into the fullness of one's humanity. In this sense the Fall is part of a natural process or progress—which Thel rejects at her peril—and also an act of faith, a confirmation of the trust that is invested in human nature.

• To pass from innocence to experience is dreadful; for Blake such a passage parallels Christ's assumption of mortality and his acceptance of the knowledge and suffering that mortality requires. In this regard alone Blake's mythmaking, even as it is evident in this one short poem, "The Little Girl Lost," is more central to the European tradition of mythic poetry than anything to be found in Collins or Gray. Even by 1789, by which time the Lyca poems were composed, Blake had come to regard innocence merely as a prelude, an early and short-lived state of the soul, and therefore, in his growing conception, associated with childhood.

Such arguments point to Blake's fundamental conception of experience: it is the state of the soul offering either potential liberation or potential enslavement. Experience may be, as it is in such songs of •*Experience* as "London," "Holy Thursday," "The Chimney Sweeper," and "The Garden of Love," identified with what Blake calls "mind-forg'd manacles." The manacles are those of which Earth speaks in the second poem of *Experience*. That they are mind-forged implies capitulation to the empirically derived facts of existence, the world of Bacon and Locke, which imprisons man within the reality of the senses and denies imagination.

In the poems cited above, the state of the soul known as experience is given its social manifestations. Injustice, suffering, poverty, and corruption are the results. But the somewhat more insidious elements of experience—insidious because hidden—are given expression in such songs as "The Clod and the Pebble," "The Sick Rose," "My Pretty Rose Tree," "A Poison Tree," and "A Little Boy Lost." In most of these poems the enemy that Blake confronts is a duplicitous pietism masking not merely selfishness but repression and the secret sense of guilt which generates repression. In the *Visions of the Daughters of Albion* Blake explores this subject, suggesting there, as in the *Songs of Experience,* that the conventional and commonplace reality, which *is* experience, provides the perfect mental factory for those manacles that enchain the human spirit.

All of these poems define the limitations of experience as a place or state of imprisonment. Within such a context mere passivity is of no use, for passivity engenders the rationalizing morality of "The Human Abstract," the conviction that

> Pity would be no more,
> If we did not make somebody Poor;
> And Mercy no more could be,
> If all were as happy as we.

The argument is the familiar one based on the proposition that partial evil equals universal good, that in a complex system of checks and balances God works in mysterious ways for the good of the whole, making occasional and necessary sacrifices of the parts to ensure the well-working of the totality. The idea is basic to the myth of experience, to human behavior founded upon such a belief; it is, after all, "the dismal shade / Of Mystery" which "bears the fruit of Deceit" and in which "the Raven his nest has made."

The true contrary to the passivity of experience, and the source of potential liberation, arises from the energies of the poet-prophet, who is himself brought into existence because of experience. And if experience is inevitable, it is far from

necessarily final. Hagstrum calls experience "blighted Innocence," adding that it is "not a period of horrible but healthy
purgation, a purgatory we must inevitably traverse en route
to the heavenly kingdom."[18] Oddly, and almost incidentally,
the passions evoked by Collins and Gray have been transformed into a set of conditions definitive of the state of experience, the spectres of the mind which arise within it. The
point at which Collins and Gray finally arrive—the delineation of those unsubstantial things—is for Blake merely a
stage in the progress of the human spirit. Herein lies Blake's
real relation to these "masters," the tutelage he has received
from them has enabled him to pass beyond them. And this
has been possible not because Blake has denied the reality of
the passions but because he has placed them within the context of recurrent temptation, that inducement to submit to a
superior power which time and nature engender within us.

In one sense, therefore, Blake reads Gray very badly, but
such a misreading is the key to his own freedom. Gray's
"ministers of fate" are the truths espoused by Theotormon,
propagated by Bromion in the service of Urizen. What are
for Gray, and the halted Collins of the odes to Pity and Fear,
the terrible and wonderful visions of the mind, are for Blake
the perils of experience. Thus his poetry is a pilgrim's progress, a journey that requires crossing fearful borders. For
Gray, as in the "Ode on a Distant Prospect of Eton College,"
the passage is ultimate, irreversible, final; terrible knowledge
is palliated in the "Elegy" by the consolations of sympathy
but embraced in "The Bard" as the high doom of the prophetic poet. For Collins, in the "Ode to Fear," Fancy lifts the veil
between the world and the world unknown. Blake suggests
that the world to which Fancy gives access is merely another
subtle and masterful delusion, a Urizenic trick of the mind, a
delusion presented as a final reality, an essence.

For Collins, as we have seen, Fear and Pity are invoked as

the sources of poetic power. For Blake such passions are not sources of energy but call forth the energy that is to do battle with them, the energy that resides in imagination. This is to turn Blake's midcentury predecessors inside out, to show them as victims of the terrors that possessed them. In the *Songs of Innocence and Experience* Blake recreates the drama of the passions; dividing them into separate states of the soul, he reveals the incompleteness of each state as each state is seen ultimately in relation to the other. For Blake the passions of experience are equivalent to Temple's "Bul-beggars" of the mind, but with one important difference. For Temple such qualities are illusions, simple fictions. For Blake they are delusions, impediments to vision that nature imposes, the materials of human trial and suffering.

The Wartons, following Addison, open the way back to the fairy way of writing. Collins and Gray body forth "unsubstantial things." Blake does something so simple that it is remarkable. He takes them seriously (even as he does Macpherson), which is to say he finds their visions probable and marvelous at once, and uses them as the building blocks of his own reconstructed image of human nature. The critical difference, where questions of influence are concerned, is that between the Blake of the *Poetical Sketches* and the Blake of the *Songs of Innocence and Experience*. The dreamy personifications of the seasonal addresses, of "To the Evening Star" and "To Morning" are in the mode of Thomson and Collins. That Blake continues to use emblematic or allegorical personification in his later works should not, however, disguise the fact that the meaning of such figures is vastly different from the meanings given those comparable personifications in the Wartons, Collins, and Gray.

Blake's assimilation of mid-century influences involves a complex relation to his predecessors. It suggests the terms by which one poetic revolution is built upon another. The passions are what Blake and Wordsworth inherited from the poets of mid-century. Blake does not deny his inheritance; he transforms it into the terms of his own vision. The passions of *Experience* are endowed with a causality that explains their inception; this is the way of myth. In *Experience* the passions are a Urizenic gift, the guilt and fear that Milton's Jehovah would bestow. Unlike Wordsworth, Blake does not attack personification because, again unlike Wordsworth, he does not see personification as an outmoded poetic heightening but as a reality of the mind. Blake therefore does not need to invent what he can derive from mid-century, but he makes a myth to account for it. He does what he says imagination does: expands the circle of reason to take in more than it had previously accommodated, and in doing so enlarges the terms of vision. This is why he is sympathetic to Gray; he reads Gray in the terms that Gray makes available to him. And when he corrects Gray he is doing for that poet the same thing that he does for Milton.

Once the problem of influence is cast into these terms, it becomes apparent that Blake's derivations from the mid-century poets constitute the terms of his reaction to them. From the standpoint of literary history it makes no difference whether Blake knew this. It makes an extraordinary difference, however, in terms of his relation to English Romanticism and suggests a way to account for the emergence of Romanticism in the last decades of the century. Such an account cannot be satisfactorily summed by retelling the arguments for an organic view of nature, the development of British empirical psychology, subjectivism, or any number of topics to which incipient Romanticism is commonly referred. When late in the century the dissenting tradition—heterodox Christianity—flooded into the passions that broke forth at mid-century, the confluence was the great renewal of English poetry we know as Romanticism.[19] One way to state this consequence is to focus briefly on the idea of the poet, as such a conception is given expression in the poetry of passion and in the surviving tradition of the religious sublime. For the mid-century romancers the poet was the exponent of feeling; for Smart, as in "A Song to David," the poet was the voice of adoration, linking the generality of mankind to the divine and in his own person bearing witness to God's continuing presence in the universe. The Romantic idea of the poet required a coalescence of both functions and, in addition, something of the Johnsonian emphasis on the poet's obligations to nature and to human nature (ordinary human experience). If we conceive of the poetry of passion, of the poetry of the religious sublime, and of Johnson, as the most formidable of the surviving eighteenth-century humanists, standing imposingly between and approving of neither, we may derive some idea of the task that confronted early Romantic poets. The difficulty involved nothing less than an elaborate accommodation of disparate and diverse values. Blake's achievement in this regard is extraordinary, and the power of his intuitive organization of heterogeneous traditions suggests his control of the immediate poetic past.

Some of what has been said here will not be unfamiliar to students of Blake, but the sorting out is necessary to suggest the terms of Blake's enterprise in relation to the poets of mid-century. The would-be mythmaking of Collins, Gray, and the Wartons is prophetic without prophecy, visionary without envisioning either a conception of human nature relevant to man's progress in the world or to the specific role of the poet as social being. Moreover such poetry is, with some exceptions, only distantly related to those great English poets of the past from whom it seeks to derive its authority. The weakly perceived realities of much of Gray's poetry offered Blake the opportunity, through his illustrations, to provide what seemed to him the true subjects of such poems.

Therefore even as early as 1789–1793 Blake was setting out the subjects of his major poetry: the myth of the Fall, the warring contrarieties of human nature, and the usurpation of true human power by the deadening influences of a debased and unimaginative Christianity. This is Blake's achievement in the *Songs;* it is a mythmaking that owes much to his real master, Milton, the subject of whose epic Blake has chosen, as his lifetime task, to reimagine and recreate.

In the gnomic poetry of *Innocence* and *Experience* Blake gave expression to a conception of human nature that had little to do with mid-century ideas of the fancy, with the merely pictorial representation of and appeal to the passions, or with cultural primitivism as an end in itself. Much of Frye's entire case for the influence of the mid-century poets upon Blake rests on the *Poetical Sketches,* but it is surely worth remembering that the poems composing this collection were written by Blake before the age of twenty, poems which, as Frye admits, he "had not bothered to revise." By 1789 the elements of "Gothic horror, the charnel house and the graveyard, primitivism, northern antiquities," and such like subjects cited by Frye as evidence of the mid-century influence, had been not so much abandoned by Blake as disciplined to serve the purposes of an enlarged and enlarging conception of a human identity both probable and marvelous. As Kathleen Raine remarks, "The influence of Collins and Gray, Rowley and Ossian, Thomson and Spenser and Shakespeare, whose literary traces are easy to discover in the early *Poetical Sketches,* could not, singly or collectively, have given Blake the necessary training in the use of symbols." Such a training Raine finds "need not be explained by literary influences at all," and she attributes Blake's growth into a symbolist poet to the supposition that he was "from his early years saturated in the atmosphere of Swedenborgian symbolism."[20]

Whatever the exact influence of Swedenborg may have been, and whatever the significance of his lapse from Swedenborgian doctrine, as the satire of that visionary in *The Marriage of Heaven and Hell* implies, it is clear that in the *Songs of Innocence and Experience* and in such other early works as *Thel* and *Tiriel*, Blake sought to embody a developing conception of man in relation to that vital fact of everyman's history, the fall from grace. The theme is not without relevance to Gray, but the distance separating his conception from Blake's is immense. Gray conceived the loss of childhood innocence, as in the "Ode on a Distant Prospect of Eton College," as lamentable, and the oncoming of experience, if we may adapt Blake's term to that poem, as a grievous reality and sore oppression of the spirit. Even childhood itself was envisioned by Gray as a period of naive deception and unknowing, to be followed by a decline and fall from which there is no redemption. His position is not unlike that of the speaker of the "Nurse's Song" of *Experience* and characteristic generally of Gray's sense of human life informed, as it was, by a melancholic desire for a kindred spirit with "soul sincere."

Blake's kindred spirit is Milton, the Milton who, in the work so titled, enters into Blake and joins with him: "And I became One Man with him arising in my strength." Gray's kindred spirit was a man of sensibility, a poet like himself, whose principal mode of vision was elegiac. The purpose of Blake's poem is to correct and recreate Milton's vision by allowing Milton to see the error that has misled him. Blake therefore suggests the necessity for reimagining Milton's epic, and by having Milton enter into him he affirms the incorporation within himself of his great progenitor. He is thus enabled to reveal Milton's limitations of vision, the misconception of the purposes of Creation that caused him to go astray.

Milton must be cured of the sickness of reason, and such sickness must stand revealed to Blake so as not to obscure the clarity of his own vision. One way therefore to regard the poem is to see it not as a development of Blake's thought (which in another way it surely is) but as an explanation of the preparations that the prophetic poet must undergo. In this sense the poem explains the relation between Blake and Milton, a relation already fruitful of the *Songs of Innocence and Experience* and the early *epyllia*. Thus *Milton* represents a doubling over the traces of Blake's own thought and an objectification in poetry of truths that were already known to him and by 1803 had found partial expression in *The Four Zoas*.

It is odd, consequently, to recall that Eliot's essay of 1920 praises Blake only to object complacently to his unfortunate distance from the "tradition" and laments that "what his genius required, and what it sadly lacked, was a framework of accepted and traditional ideas which would have prevented him from indulging in a philosophy of his own." And it is interesting to find Eliot making a comment similar to Arnold's earlier observation about Gray: "The fault is perhaps not with Blake himself, but with the environment which failed to provide what such a poet needed."[21]

Blake's mythmaking, what Frye calls his allegory, is very different from what the critics and poets of mid-century England understood by allegory. For them allegory was primarily an embodiment of the unseen, of the unbodied finding expression in the delineation of the passions. This is the conception governing Collins's odes, and it is what Thomas Warton meant when he praised Spenser's allegory. In referring to the subjects of his odes as descriptive and allegorical Collins did not so much signify a difference between the descriptive and allegorical as he did a similarity. The descriptive was the allegorical, for such qualities as Pity, Fear, and

Simplicity were bodied forth in personifications iconographically embellished. The method of heightened pictorialism permitted the reader to see, as he would in a painting, qualities that were otherwise unavailable to vision. But this is not the method of myth, for myth is concerned with origins and the explanation of these qualities. The passions of experience are the agents of the Miltonic myth reinterpreted by Blake. No song of *Experience* more boldly sets forth what Blake calls "vision," his mythmaking, than "A Poison Tree."

The poem begins in the fact of disagreement with someone, a "foe," and the speaker nourishes a hatred which, locked up within him, grows within. The foe is compelled to "eat" of the imprisoned emotion, and the evil that thereby springs outward into existence finds its object in the fallen body of the enemy. In experience life is corrupted by repression. Blake's speaker is so corrupted and shares in the common condition of the fallen world. The poem uncovers the archetype of the wrathful one within him, the Satanic figure of the Edenic garden, whose deceit, like the tree of "The Human Abstract," grows steadily within. Like Satan the speaker has perverted Creation; his crime is the Satanic one of rage acting through hypocrisy for the purposes of negation. From the central symbol of the tree radiates the entire complex of the archetype: the forbidden fruit, the garden, the intruder, deceit, and death; in sum, the fallen state of man in a fallen world. The material form of experience is the tree that grows in the human brain.

As myth the poem does not merely point to an action that took place at some prior time or summon the emotions attendant upon the action. The myth is the form and the action; from the standpoint of Blake's radical Christianity that is the eternal form. All behavior founded on deceit, hypocrisy, and temptation recreates this form, Blake is saying, because the event is the form, and there can be no such reality as a true event independent of its eternal form. Here is where Blake most decidedly parts company, for example, with Reynolds. For Reynolds form is an abstraction, an idea built up from close observation of nature and seized by the artist when he reflects on the impressions with which his mind is stored. For Blake all true observation is form because perception is not divided into parts but is itself a unity. The mind does not see and then think any more than it particularizes in order to generalize. The particularity is the generalization.

The poets and critics of mid-century consistently associated allegory with the marvelous, with the "terrible graces of magic and enchantment." When Warton praised the poetry of the late sixteenth century he did so largely because in that period he found a compromise between the incredible fictions of romance and the elegant, sophisticated art of the English Augustans. Warton's compromise—"civilized superstition"—points to the problem. The marvelous was necessary if the passions were to be engaged, if admiration was to be awakened. But, on the other hand, to be moved by the merely marvelous suggested a degree of credulity disturbing to civilized man.

Taking his lead from Addison, Hurd proposed that the marvelous is not unnatural as it appeals to the buried beliefs of human nature. And while the real question of the purposes of allegory (or myth) was left unanswered, and even unraised, most mid-century critics were generally more comfortable with Milton than with Ariosto or Tasso because what was most marvelous in Milton was not the result of pagan superstition, but Christian revelation. Where the occasion of the marvelous was not sacred poetry, however, the mid-century critics duly and commonly accepted the enchantment of the reason.

The criterion of fine fabling inevitably introduced the

subject of probability. By taking their subjects from either popular belief or legend both Collins and Gray narrowly observed a credible basis for the fabulous, but the "Ode on the Popular Superstitions" and "The Bard" necessarily promoted the values of cultural primitivism. Yet, to come full circle, primitive poetry (witness Blair on Ossian and Addison on "Chevy Chase") was not without the sanction of nature. To neglect the past was to diminish human nature, which was itself a product of the past.

The conviction rested on something akin to a principle of psychological plenitude: human nature was various and capacious. Even the sophisticated mind contained a darker underside which yearned to see represented the images lurking in its shadows. The more extreme expression of this conviction celebrated obscurity: "our ignorance . . . causes all our admiration, and chiefly excites our passions. . . . The mind is hurried out of itself, by a croud of great and confused images; which affect because they are crouded and confused."[22] But if the extreme position was seldom followed, it was nevertheless consistent with an increasing tolerance for a broad, and by Augustan standards, enthusiastic appeal to the imagination.

Yet Blake had little in common with the psychological tradition in eighteenth-century criticism. He was not interested merely in sensations and with good reason, for they led only to the dead end of a poetically unusable psychologizing, the distant product of those cosmic and mental mechanics Blake detested. The implications of associational psychology led to sustained debate in the middle and later years of the eighteenth century over the relative merits of painting, poetry, and music conceived as sources of impressions upon the mind. The remote and antique, the legendary and fabulous, could be justified as highly usable subjects in relation to the new psychology, and the entire question of poetic probability, or improbability, be referred to the cognitive purposes of art. Thus in the middle years of the century, when attention had shifted to faculty psychology and to inquiries into genius, imagination, taste, and related topics, the imagination was commonly regarded as "that faculty whereby the mind not only reflects on its own operations, but which assembles the various ideas conveyed to the understanding by the canal of sensation, and treasured up in the repository of memory, compounding or disjoining them at pleasure; and which, by its plastic power of inventing new associations of ideas, and of combining them with infinite variety, is enabled to present a creation of its own, and to exhibit scenes and objects which never existed in nature."[23] On this basis poetic license was liberty without measure, and, in William Duff's terms, literary illusion was justified by the mental makeup of the artist resembling a jigsaw puzzle. When the pieces fell into place the result was a work of art. Yet such recipes had long been a part of neoclassic epistemology, and it was not too long a return journey from here to Hobbes's pronouncement on the ingredients necessary to make a poem: "Time and Education begets Experience; Experience begets memory; Memory begets Judgement and Fancy: Judgement begets the strength and structure, and Fancy begets the ornaments of a Poem."[24]

Beginning with what was derived from nature (images conveyed through sensation) the artist arranged the images into new combinations. To Blake such an idea of the artist would have seemed trifling and insignificant. In Lavater's *Aphorisms on Man* the following statement occurs: "The greatest of characters, no doubt, was he, who, free of all trifling accidental helps, could see objects through one grand immutable medium, always at hand, and proof against illusion and time, reflected by every object, and invariably traced through all the fluctuation of things." Blake's comment is simply: "this was Christ."[25] As the introductory poem of *Experience* makes clear, Christ's voice is the voice that the bard has heard ("Whose ears have heard / The Holy Word"), and he speaks with the same liberating impulse that governs the Holy Word. The bard knows, or aspires to know, what Christ knows, for the true poet's life is a listening to the Word and a cleansing of perception, a driving out of those idols of the mind that threaten to take possession of our humanity.

Moreover the paradigm for innocence-experience-higher innocence is derived from the Christ who descended from heaven, assumed flesh, died, and rose again. Having willingly accepted the state of experience he has therefore "traced through all the fluctuation of things." In *There Is No Natural Religion* Blake says, "Therefore God becomes as we are, that we may be as he is"; and in *All Religions Are One,* "the forms of all things are derived from their Genius." As the "Religions of all Nations are derived from each Nation's different reception of the Poetic Genius which is every where call'd the Spirit of Prophecy," the only possible image of human life has "one source." Finally, "the true Man is the source he being the Poetic Genius."[26] Herein lies the triumph of Blake's myth, rooted in the conviction that Jesus and the poet are one and the same person and that the true bard recreates in his life the radical vision of Christ.

By 1788–1789 Blake had passed beyond his earliest formative influences, and his use of them resides in the formulation and reconstruction of the comprehensive myth of man and God. In Blake, as in Wordsworth, the poetic vision derives from a rebuilding of those truths that permanently inhere in human nature, those that are, in the conception of each poet, central to human life. In Blake, through the poetic genius the marvelous is shown to be most probable. The piper and the bard are each an aspect of the poetic genius, whose purpose is to reveal the divine within the human, the

human as divine. Blake states in the "Annotations to Lavater," "human nature is the image of God." In the "Annotations to Swedenborg," where Swedenborg remarks that "the
Negation of God constitutes Hell, and in the Christian World
the Negation of the Lord's Divinity," Blake writes in response: "the Negation of the Poetic Genius." The "Poetic
Genius . . . is the Lord."[27]

When the speaker of "The Tyger" envisions the tiger as
dreadful he is merely envisioning and projecting into nature
his own fear of the God he himself has created, which in effect
is his own fear of himself. The speaker has created an image
of man that is dreadful because he does not want man to
behave in a certain way, the way of revolutionary energy.
That way is fearful to all who live complacently within experience. What is seemingly outside man—the tiger—is really
inside, as inside as the tree of the knowledge of good and evil:

> The Gods of the earth and sea,
> Sought thro' Nature to find this Tree
> But their search was all in vain:
> There grows one in the Human Brain.

When man concocts the story of the tree and places it
outside himself, we are reminded by Blake's poem that the
tree's first location was internal.[28] To write in such a way is to
construct—*reconstruct* would be the better word, given
Blake's primary sources in the Bible and Miltonic epic—the
endurable image of human nature. Blake could have agreed
with Wordsworth when the latter called for a poetry of subjects that permanently affect mankind, although they would
not often have agreed in their visions of such subjects. Both
poets have often been thought enraptured and therefore
fabulous. But each sought to restore to poetry both its fundamental wonder and probability, the specific probability of
human act and belief viewed in relation to those subjects that
lie at the center of consciousness. In this regard Blake locates

the evidence for God not in nature but in man. And to this should be added that the evidence for both God and Satan is to be found in man. Such evidence constitutes a system of sorts, but it is a system of mind, an anatomy or grammar of motives and countermotives that sponsors the oppositions and the warfare within, the militant vision of man struggling to realize not merely his passions but the god within.

5
William Wordsworth

Let us begin by asking what is the most perilous activity in which a poet can engage? The answer probably is the deliberate creation of that which is imaginatively inaccessible to his audience. The great risk run by the new writer is that he fall outside what has been recognizably important to his readers. If his audience is serious and cultivated and the writer is outside and above, his reputation is unlikely to suffer. When he falls outside and below, however, he is in trouble. This is what happened to Wordsworth, in the judgment of his readers, often enough to make this fact a worthwhile one with which to begin this inquiry. The difficulty for many reviewers of Wordsworth's early lyrics is that he was too low, too natural in feeling and expression, too undiscriminating to engage the serious reader.

When Francis Jeffrey mocked the "particular character" narrating "The Thorn" ("A pale man in a green coat—sitting cross-legged on an oaken stool—with a scratch on his nose, and a spelling dictionary on the table")[1] he meant that some information is unnecessary and some is despicable because it calls attention to what is below serious consideration. It is easy enough to say now what Wordsworth had in view. He wanted us to recognize the determinations that previous experience imposes upon perception. This may seem, however, to result in creating a cult of special experience. But what is often involved is a heightened form of psychological realism, a literature that frequently approaches the terms of a dramatic case study. The poet or his surrogate is subjected to unusually unsettling experiences arising from what may appear initially as a rather ordinary occasion. The formula is: nothing is below suspicion; everything is valuable, particularly the obvious. But if we accept the premise that Wordsworth was interested in creating new experience, then he had to begin with what was neglected previously. That is, he had to begin with what is below ordinary experience, below in the sense of insufficient importance as well as in the psychological sense of that which lies underneath. Both meanings come together in the proposition that from the insignificant the significant arises. Therefore we often have a poetry concentrated on arisings. And this prepares us for the tone of expectancy that frequently characterizes his verse, the air of something about to happen.

We may recognize in this tone one of the contrivances of Wordsworth's verse, a strategy by which the poet commemorates the spontaneous moment, but we should also recognize the form in which factual notations are made. Wordsworth's "five years," "five summers," "five long winters!" initiate a pattern of recognition and repetition which the poem embodies. We may think of this as a matter of tracking the mind, setting it in the mental grooves that it will follow in the poem. The notations are those of fact, but the form of the notation implies a psychology. The relation here between the representation of a fact and mental form suggests a very narrow but profound innovation in Wordsworth's poetry. His mind acts in and through the texture of observation and fact; more characteristically the eighteenth-century poet thinks categorically and dualistically. Ralph Cohen cites the 1726 critic who declared that Thomson had shown "a *new* and *masterly manner* in which he has introduced his reflections, and made them to succeed his several Descriptions." As late as 1784 Cowper explained his achievements in *The Task* in similar terms: "My descriptions are all from nature. . . . My delineations of the heart are from my own experience."[2] The discrimination between observation and thought results in qualities being built up from the outside rather than from the inside.

The fact has several consequences. One is that the eighteenth-century lyric tends toward the presentation of qualities or states of mind by endowing them circumstantially, by offering the emblems of an affective presence. Personification is the most immediate mode of such representation. Oliver Sigworth suggests of Collins's ode that " 'Fear' is an allegoric subject and also a descriptive subject, because, as personified, it describes—literally 'writes down'—the emotion for us to see and vicariously to experience."[3] The poem is intended to have a direct and powerful emotional appeal, and the poet's intentions are reinforced by the density or solidity of detail that informs the figure and embellishes its context. But the emotional appeal is occasioned by the literal embellishments of the figure. This mode of representation is pictorial, for the figure is detached from its germinating occasion, from its causal relation to the psychology of the speaker. The later eighteenth-century writer was extremely interested in effects of this kind. Elizabeth Manwaring quotes William Gilpin on the changing pictures of the landscape seen through a Claude glass: "They are like the visions of the imagination; or the brilliant landscapes of a dream. Forms, and colours, in brightest array, fleet before us."[4] Such effects induce affective states; they become ways of creating experience and they go far toward signifying states of being not otherwise immediately accessible ("landscapes of a dream"), but they cannot clarify the mind's self-experience.

Under more controlled circumstances, as in a poem, the rapidly changing images can evoke a range of related emotions associated with a particular quality. Consider the opening lines of James Grainger's "Solitude":

> O Solitude, romantic maid,
> Whether by nodding towers you tread,
> Or haunt the desart's trackless gloom,
> Or hover o'er the yawning tomb,
> Or climb the Andes' clifted side,
> Or by the Nile's coy source abide,
> Or, starting from your half-year's sleep,
> From Hecla view the thawing deep,
> Or at the purple dawn of day,
> Tadmor's marble wastes survey;
>   You, recluse, again I woo,
>   And again your steps pursue.

The poet is interested in Solitude as a multivalent presence, as a quality connecting a range of varied emotional tones. The quality (Solitude) inhabits a set of local conditions, which in turn establish her emotional possibilities for the reader. Solitude is, variously, sublime, gothic, picturesque. The descriptive terms define an emotive structure, very much as an eighteenth-century tourist like Thomas West would plan his travel route so that it "leads from what is pleasing, to what is surprising; from the delicate touches of Claude . . . to the noble scenes of Poussin . . . to the stupendous romantic ideas of Salvator Rosa."[5]

From Addison to Alison eighteenth-century critics had been interested in such structures. Archibald Alison as late as 1790 suggested that "by means of the Connexion, or Resemblance, which subsists between the qualities of Matter, and qualities capable of producing Emotion, the perception of the one immediately, and very often irresistibly, suggests the idea of the other." He looked, that is, to the associations formed between "certain sensations and certain qualities," and his principles led to the idea that a work of art is an arrangement of affective patterns which constitute the structure of the work: structure is an organization of qualities designed to evoke certain sensations. In sum: "the qualities of matter become significant to us of those qualities of mind which are destined to affect us with pleasing or interesting emotion."[6] Alison was the first to formulate these principles, but they are hardly radical in relation to the psychological current of eighteenth-century aesthetics. The beautiful, the picturesque, and the sublime were predicated upon psychological principles, and the procedure of descriptive-allegorical poetry in the later period often bore a resemblance to Alison's idea of affective structures. The result was a literature consciously devoted to exploiting the feelings, and it would be difficult to think of any poetry, be it Romantic or not, more deliberately concerned with such exploitation. The differences, therefore, between the late eighteenth-century and early Romantic lyric do not depend upon questions of feeling, as such, nor upon an appeal to the validity of experience. The very strategy of the earlier descriptive poem, partially implicit at least in the use of the ubiquitous "or" (of which Grainger's ode is a striking example), defines an affective use of locale. The device of alternate locales is a way of extending nonmetaphorically the emotional implications of the quality.

Thomas Warton, in "The Pleasures of Melancholy," introduced Contemplation as alternately gothic or sublime, the "or" serving to connect the habitations of the figure and so extend her variety. The normal tendency of eighteenth-century verse was to keep separate states separate; we seldom experience the lingering resonance of one state of mind acting upon another as it forms, seldom experience the dissolution of an emotion and the strangely variegated qualities of mind involved. These observations call attention to what seems distinctive of the lyric as practiced by Wordsworth and also by Coleridge: the interest in the time-fragments separating discrete emotional states, those formative moments that inhabit the interlude between completed sequences.

Hazlitt said of poetry that it "represents forms chiefly as they suggest other forms; feelings, as they suggest forms or other feelings."[7] Hazlitt's is a fine formula and adaptable to eighteenth-century poetry so long as *other* is not taken to mean opposite or contradictory. Many later eighteenth-century poets, such as Gray in the "Ode on a Distant Prospect of Eton College," built bridges between radically different awarenesses, but they did not deliberately confound feelings with their opposites, for the reason that it was a confusing kind of activity and not likely to improve the strength or intensity of feeling. Such cautions as these, however, are not incompatible with approving tragicomedy, as Johnson did, on the grounds that alternations and vicissitudes are experientially sound. The type of proposition I have in mind, at least initially, is darker and deeper and involves the Romantic invocation of an unexpected kinship between opposites.

Wordsworth's poetry often seems meant to be puzzling because it deals in unanticipated evocations; feelings, as they suggest forms or other feelings. What is generally involved is the gradual translation of the object from its objective status to its symbolic status; in the process a feeling that exists below becomes attached to the object and is drawn out by it. As a form of homeopathic medicine or self-therapy, a purgation of previously undefined anxieties, it comes about by allowing the object to work unimpededly on the mind. The object, initially neutral or associated with one set of feelings, turns out to be pulling forth a very different set of feelings. The formula is the same as before: the obvious has marvelous powers of revelation. "Strange Fits of Passion" works in this way; the moon draws forth the lover's previously undisclosed and unrecognized feelings. Nature's influence is efficacious not only because nature is good but because nature and its objects have power over, and intimate relation to, the mind of man. In this there is something of an old magic, and Wordsworth was still reading himself in the heavens.

As a poetic device the Romantic use of the object is valuable for disclosing a set of shadow emotions, what we might call the malign forms of benign emotions. Kenneth Burke is ingenious in reading the "dialectical opposites" of the drug problem in "Kubla Khan,"[8] but the poet's strategies for exploring dialectical opposites are frequent in Coleridge's poetry, drug problem or no. Through such oppositions various relations can be symbolized: the elements that make up an opposition can meet and synthesize (Coleridge's imagery of the eye brings opposites together), or they can meet and cross (Christabel and Geraldine transfer identities after they embrace). "Christabel" itself presents an interesting example of the Coleridgean dialectic between states of innocence and experience. At the opening of the work the maiden Christabel has left the castle to pray beneath an old oak "for the weal of her lover that's far away." On the other side of the oak she shortly discovers the moaning lady Geraldine as she has been left by the five warriors. Christabel's prayer for her lover is symptomatic of an uncomplicated maidenly devotion, an innocent sexuality. In the person of Geraldine, the oak discloses its other side, its malign referent, a sexuality corrupted and perverse. Christabel's discovery is the burden she bears throughout the poem, and the specific challenge to her is that of absorbing the dialectical opposites of passion for which she is unable to find a synthesizing principle. One might go so far as to say that the poem remained unfinished because Coleridge could not himself synthesize those conflicts within his own consciousness for which the narrative is a complex symbol; many scholars have not been reluctant to draw this conclusion.

An interesting example of the unexpected emergence of an opposition occurs in "The Nightingale." After the poem opens by dispelling the associations between melancholy and nightingales, the third and fourth stanzas of the poem present in disguised form the father–maiden situation of "Christabel"

("The Nightingale" was written between attempts at the longer poem), but those initial associations will not stay down. The imagery of the nightingales' "bright, bright eyes" is linked vaguely to the serpentine "glow-worm in the shade" lighting up her "love-torch." The lady of the poem "glides through the pathways" recalling in her motion the figures of Christabel and Geraldine. The nightingale and the serpent cross in the imagery of brightness and meet again later in the poem with striking biographical revelation in the figure of Coleridge's child, whose "fair eyes" did "glitter in the yellow moon-beam." If the poem is an attempt to exorcise Coleridge's melancholia occasioned by his domestic situation (as it well may be) it was not very successful. But leaving such questions aside, the poem is a good example of the way in which malign emotions are summoned by Coleridge's imagery, pulling hidden feelings out from their habitation in the recesses of the mind.

Much of Coleridge's poetry, particularly the "conversation poems," customarily works in this way. At issue are getting down into and dramatizing the fears and compulsions of which self-consciousness is made. Non sequiturs, like Coleridge's "And" which begins the third stanza, signal the emotional dislocation of the speaker, indicating that the emotions evoked by the image pattern have begun to take over, following a logic of their own that is now using the prior terms of discourse (the imagery of the eye) as the instrumental terms of its own enactment:

> And I know a grove
> Of large extent, hard by a castle huge,
> Which the great lord inhabits not; and so
> This grove is wild with tangling underwood,
> And the trim walks are broken up, and grass,
> Thin grass and king-cups grow within the paths.
> But never elsewhere in one place I knew
> So many nightingales; and far and near,

In wood and thicket, over the wide grove,
They answer and provoke each other's song.
With skirmish and capricious passagings,
And murmurs musical and swift jug jug,
And one low piping sound more sweet than all—
Stirring the air with such a harmony,
That should you close your eyes, you might almost
Forget it was not day! On moonlight bushes,
Whose dewy leaflets are but half-disclosed,
You may perchance behold them on the twigs,
Their bright, bright eyes, their eyes both bright and full,
Glistening, while many a glow-worm in the shade
Lights up her love-torch.   (ll. 49–69)

The effect is that of setting a subconsciousness free, allowing to come to the surface an undercurrent of the speaker's emotional life that seizes upon the terms of his prior, more controlled, perceptions. It is this sense of an underlife of emotion—not the same as that present on the surface of the mind but related to it as the malign is related to the salubrious—that provides Romantic verse with some of its peculiar resonances.

This relationship is not always very neat or apparent. Coleridge commonly employs motifs of dialectic and transformation, and his willingness to exploit contrary tendencies within his own character often gives the conversation poems their special vitality. "The Eolian Harp" is one interesting example of his rejection of dangerous perceptions, "shapings of the unregenerate mind," in favor of the simplistic emblems of "Innocence and Love" ("white-flower'd Jasmin and the broad-leav'd Myrtle") stifling the marital cottage. The "midway slope" on which he reclines halfway in his reflections suggests a pause between the perilous summit of fully acknowledged recognitions and the "humble walk" of a picturesque domesticity. In the poem "vain Philosophy's aye-babbling spring" is an element as demonic or malign (under Sara's tutelage) as the river Alph is "sacred" in "Kubla Khan."

It seems quite possible that the latter poem answers the former and that "pensive Sara" finds her later place among the fearful gallery crying "Beware! Beware!"

More to the point, however, is the way in which Coleridge brings both elements into play, dramatizing the split within personality, the distance between the social being and the poet. He says as much in the Preface to the third edition of his *Poems on Various Subjects* (1803): "If I could judge of others by myself, I should not hesitate to affirm that the most interesting passages in our most interesting Poems are those in which the author develops his own feelings." The conversational poem is a fine example of a sustained Augustan mode because the reflective intimacy of the form permits a seemingly relaxed encounter with what Josephine Miles calls "the individual's lyric story, half articulated and half heard, but powerful in its force of implication."[9]

Admittedly, many of the poems in Collins's *Odes on Several Descriptive and Allegoric Subjects* suggest his willingness to engage dangerous knowledge, but even at its most impassioned, later eighteenth-century poetry seldom or never approximates the conditions just described. Instead such poetry verges on the psychologically primitive or becomes oracular. If I understand Northrop Frye, such a psychological state involves the suspension of the normal, customary identity of the poet, what Frye refers to as his "social personality." But even if this is the case, for more poets than only Chatterton and Macpherson, the distinction never becomes a function of the speaker's experiential situation in the poem. This is to say that we are seldom, if ever, confronted with an occasion where the conflict between oracular poet and social personality is dramatized by the poet in the poem. It is certainly true that eighteenth-century criticism was opposed to the dissociation of the personality as a subject for poetry. Hugh Blair was typical in calling for "a collection of strong expressive images, which are all of one class." This emphasis sometimes tended to make the representation of emotions in later eighteenth-century verse seem (at least from a nineteenth-century point of view) insincere. A.S.P. Woodhouse makes the interesting comment upon Collins's odes that "the personified qualities which form the subjects of his odes, or which are repeatedly involved in them, are treated descriptively, and whatever else of description the poems contain is devoted to providing the setting for these *personae* or to reinforcing their symbolic and emotional effect."[10] In sum, then, a series of miniature portraits: the local settings which the poet constructs for his qualities may be extensive, but the settings only sustain the emotion descriptively and provide various objective habitations for it.

Yet quite clearly the eighteenth-century poet expected his descriptions to produce strong emotional responses in the reader. One difference between late eighteenth-century and early Romantic procedures resides in the Romantic's greater willingness to risk the bifurcation of consciousness, the threat to the total personality in its involvement with an experience that may have too many surprises in store. The earlier poetry almost never suggested this risk even though the intensity of the poet's response may at times have become, as Frye suggests, and as is the case with the "stricken deer" passage in *The Task,* manic or bizarre. At issue is the special challenge to the whole personality which Wordsworth and Coleridge liked to dramatize, and which corresponds inversely to that special sort of connectedness among the differing aspects of experience which they liked equally to emphasize. More characteristically the Wartons, Collins, and Gray preferred to shift attention to the emotion itself as something detachable and apart from the percipient with its own independent life. The emotion is thus richly figured in the sense that it is dressed up iconographically, given what Ricardo Quintana calls "a certain existential quality."[11] The somewhat static quality of the representation is justified by its pictorial richness. Apparently the eighteenth-century reader took a special satisfaction in recognizing what an emotion looked like; he wanted to be able to see it, and the satisfactions of the tableau vivant are those of a portrait gallery in miniature. But even when such was obviously not the case, as in the *Olney Hymns,* our attention is directed to a special state of sensibility, a particular condition of emotional receptivity or vulnerability, rather than to a mental process.

The best way to control something with which we are uneasy may be to ridicule it (Shaftesbury's test, but not Johnson's); the next best way is to give in to it, cultivate it, as the later eighteenth-century poets and novelists cultivated the gothic and the terrible sublime. One method dispels the mysterious; the other perhaps too generously gratifies our desire for it. Thomas Warton, for example, plunged the reader into the semblances of melancholy; so effectively are we exposed to the catalogue of possibilities comprised by melancholy that we are hardly aware that the emotion has no problematical relation to the emotional life. By being made into an object of contemplation the place of melancholy in the emotional life of the reader is fixed and halted. Later eighteenth-century poets cultivated this effect so often that through it they created their own special cult of sensibility or feeling. But it is possible to suspect that a cult of sensibility arises when something is felt to be wrong with the emotional life, and cultism is another way of pacifying powers too dangerous to be left alone. When emotions are given a special status in nature they are effectively raised above the individual life. The logic is: feeling, as such, is more important than what I feel; since this is so it is best not to be too particular about my own feelings, and, in any event, my feelings are one small part of the universe of feeling. Thus one surrenders not to one's own emotions but to feeling itself. But if what one feels is more or less suspect, then perhaps it is possible to tap some sort of universe of emotion. Frye adopts Rimbaud's "on me pense" to comment on the process of oracular composition in later eighteenth-century poetry, to explain "some of the identifications involving the poet."[12] But what are these identities if not displacements of one's ordinary identity for the sake of feelings higher (in the sense of *above*) than those available to one's ordinary identity?

There are many indications in the eighteenth century of a sustained seeking after strong emotions, after the vast, the dreadful, the grand, the sublime, the awful, the lofty. Sometimes what was called for was deceiving the reason in sudden thrills of emotion "before the intellectual Power, Reason, can descend from the Throne of the Mind to ratify it's Approbation."[13] Sometimes a kind of helter-skelter activity was encouraged by images that "crowd on each other" to produce a "continued hurry of surprise,"[14] and sometimes it was just the sheer pleasure of imaginative freedom, as when "scenes or objects [are shown] which never existed in nature."[15] Or the poet learned to speak like a Celtic or medieval bard and so mimicked the heroic by speaking in a key well above his own immediate experience. All these excitations were better because above. Moreover, the Augustans, in Monk's words, "grouped the stronger emotions and the more irrational elements of art" into the *sublime,* leaving the *beautiful* as the antithesis to it; in the view of Burke's recent editor, J. T. Boulton, the latter was merely "a weak and sentimentalized conception"; in Ernst Cassirer's view, a phenomenon limited solely to "teaching the proper forms of social intercourse and . . . refining morals."[16] Among the recognizable signs of the true sublime was the immediately transporting effect it produced upon the beholder; it raised him to an awareness of the grandeur in and beyond natural objects.

After so many had gone so far it was difficult to go further. What we might expect from the new poet, then, is not a refinement of the principles of *Peri Hupsous* (*On the Sublime*) but a different way of investing the descriptive particular with emotive resonance. Wordsworth tends to moralize the virtues of rural existence as a way of guarding against the charge of dealing in eccentricities. Character becomes for him the vehicle whereby he communicates his major subject, his "true realism," as Geoffrey Hartman remarks, "the powers man struggles with in his progress toward self-consciousness."[17] Such powers are those that the object, invested with human form, imposes upon the self-seeking imagination. In this regard the imagination recreates itself through its engagement with the object to give us an image or objectification of its own processes. "The Thorn" is a notable example of this effort in Wordsworth's poetry.

If we think of character as a way of objectifying the imaginative process, we can perceive that for Wordsworth the function of character is similar, if not analogous, to that which landscape may serve—the making patent an awareness of *another*. In the few poems that comprise the "Poems on the Naming of Places" there is one called "To M.H."

> Our walk was far among the ancient trees:
> There was no road, nor any woodman's path;
> But a thick umbrage—checking the wild growth
> Of weed and sapling, along the soft green turf
> Beneath the branches—of itself had made
> A track, that brought us to a slip of lawn,
> And a small bed of water in the woods.
> All round this pool both flocks and herds might drink
> On its firm margin, even as from a well,
> Or some stone-basin which the herdsman's hand
> Had shaped for their refreshment; nor did sun,
> Or wind from any quarter, ever come,
> But as a blessing to this calm recess,
> This glade of water and this one green field.

The spot was made by Nature for herself;
The travellers know it not, and 'twill remain
Unknown to them; but it is beautiful;
And if a man should plant his cottage near,
Should sleep beneath the shelter of its trees,
And blend its waters with his daily meal,
He would so love it, that in his death-hour
Its image would survive among his thoughts:
And therefore, my sweet Mary, this still Nook,
With all its beeches, we have named from You!

The M.H. to whom the poem is addressed is Mary Hutchinson, and the poem was written shortly before she became Wordsworth's wife. Ostensibly the subject of the poem is the discovery and description of a special place in nature, unknown to travellers, which Wordsworth dedicates to Mary. I say the ostensible subject because the real subject of the poem is Wordsworth's experience of Mary to which the form of the poem corresponds. Description is the translation of the disclosed being of Mary Hutchinson, as Wordsworth knows his awareness of her, into the objectifications of landscape. In the action of disclosure the poet's eye regards the contours of the mind's self-experience. The place, as Wordsworth tells us, is not named *for* Mary, but *from* her, *from* signifying in context exactly that transposition of being into landscape which the poet strives to achieve. The landscape is invested with human form, is a vestment of consciousness, and, reciprocally, makes patent to the poet his knowledge of Mary. It is odd therefore to recall that even where the *Lyrical Ballads* had been generously praised, Wordsworth was criticized for his "knack of feeling about subjects with which feeling had no proper concern."[18]

But the very similarity of penseroso moments in later eighteenth-century verse suggests that the subjective intensity of such moments was highly qualified by conventional terms of discourse. A cluster of scenes from Warton, Beattie,

Collins, and Goldsmith makes for a typically melancholy composition and all speakers merge in the generalized voice of the gothic mode:

> Beneath yon ruin'd abbey's moss-grown piles
> Oft let me sit, at twilight hour of eve,
> Where thro' some western window the pale moon
> Pours her long-levell'd rule of streaming light;
> While sullen sacred silence reigns around,
> Save the lone screech-owl's note, who builds his bow'r
> Amid the mould'ring caverns dark and damp,
> Or the calm breeze, that rustles in the leaves
> Of flaunting ivy, that with mantle green
> Invests some wasted tow'r.
> ("The Pleasures of Melancholy," ll. 28–37)

> When the long-sounding curfew from afar
> Loaded with loud lament the lonely gale,
> Young Edwin, lighted by the evening star,
> Lingering and listening, wander'd down the vale,
> There would he dream of graves, and corses pale;
> And ghosts that to the charnel-dungeon throng,
> And drag a length of clanking chain, and wail,
> Till silenced by the owl's terrific song,
> Or blast that shrieks by fits the thundering isles along.
> (*The Minstrel,* I, ll. 280–88)

> With Eyes up-rais'd, as one inspir'd,
> Pale *Melancholy* sate retir'd,
> And from her wild sequester'd Seat,
> In Notes by Distance made more sweet,
> Pour'd thro' the mellow *Horn* her pensive Soul.
> ("The Passions," ll. 57–61)

> Those matted woods where birds forget to sing,
> But silent bats in drowsy clusters cling,
> Those poisonous fields with rank luxuriance crowned
> Where the dark scorpion gathers death around;
> Where at each step the stranger fears to wake
> The rattling terrors of the vengeful snake.
> ("The Deserted Village," ll. 349–54)

The point of this extensive quoting is not to prove that these poets were imitating one another. They were satisfying a particular standard of sensibility, but one that did not, within the mode, make for much variety or flexibility. The descriptive possibilities of the scene and the qualities it betokens are both filled and fulfilled. Eighteenth-century critical theory did not lead beyond these possibilities, even though the evident interest in *suggestiveness* rendered through incompleteness and obscurity implies an attempt "to disclose what is beyond the formal quality of the object."[19] While Archibald Alison suggested that beyond the formal quality are the associations with which it is imbued, the implications of a loosely determined particular remained largely unexplored. And with good reason, for suggestiveness stood at the limit of what was permitted by eighteenth-century critical tolerance. The language of metaphor may be so conceived as to permit the private sensibility a respite from its public functions but in any event no sustained and problematical relation between the private and public areas was encouraged. Therefore the voices speaking the passages quoted above suggest only highly generalized characters speaking of private sensations in public tones. Such passages hold the conventional tones of the descriptive or allegorical lyric, tones which may modulate through the scale into the picturesque dialect of a Fergusson or Burns without disturbing the fundamental relation between private and public sensibility.

But if we ask what a young man in the 1790s might do to make a name for himself, the obvious answer is that he might look around to see what had been neglected or undervalued and start with that. Crabbe had gained something of a reputation when still a young man by satirizing rural pleasures, while Blake, less publicly successful, had moved toward a new pastoral in the *Poetical Sketches*. Crabbe was praised for his truthful delineations of village life, but Wordsworth was often chided not only for using the language of the lower classes but for the improbability of his characterizations. Byron, reviewing in *Monthly Literary Recreations,* complained of Wordsworth's "abandoning his mind to the most common-place ideas, at the same time clothing them in language not simple, but puerile."[20] If the criticism is harsh, it is that Byron like many others, including Hazlitt on occasion, could not envision anything useful coming from what seemed an exceptional interest in the mental vagaries of uninteresting and uncultivated people. Even what was sometimes regarded as Wordsworth's "rapturous mysticism"[21] was frequently regarded as the unintelligible product of interests too low to justify or make clear the poet's vision.

Earlier I discussed the way in which later eighteenth-century writers liked to deploy the representation of emotions, the strategies by which the poet imposed his authority and justified his knowledge of the subject. Collins's "Ode to Pity" offers an illustrative example. Pity comes forth evoked by Distress. Pity is robed in blue; she has been heard by Ilissus and Arun; she has soothed Echo. The poet promises to raise a temple to Pity with "Picture's Toils." Finally he will retire there, "Allow'd with Thee to dwell." Introducing himself into the scene, the poet proclaims his relation to Pity and announces his authority: he knows what is owing to Pity; he has the credentials to be the proper, because sympathetic, celebrant. Collins's authority is formidable, not because the poem is an enactment of his knowing but because like a true companion and intimate of Pity he knows her well. The poet is chronicler, architect, designer, and companion. If we ask why all this is necessary, the answer is that something has gone wrong with British poetry and Pity has lost interest in it:

There waste the mournful lamp of night,
Till, virgin, thou again delight
To hear a British shell!

The ending of the poem tells us what we suspected all
along: feeling exists independently of its causes and is the
excuse for its own existence. The purpose of the poem is to
build up an affective presence, not to dispraise British poetry.
But the construction of such a presence separates emotions
from the context of kindred emotions within the mind and
obviates a problematical relation between the emotion and
those responses it may evoke from the speaker. Instead, the
emotion, pity, is projected into its pictorial form; it thereby
assumes a separate status as an object independent of the poet
from whose imagination it has presumably issued. Once
emotions are separated from the speaker in this way they are
no longer determinants of his self-consciousness. They lose
their power as occasions of conflict or contradiction within
his personality, and the more complete the separation the less
critical, and therefore the less dramatic, the challenge to the
speaker's self-awareness.

On the other hand, Wordsworth and Coleridge often build
bridges ("pontificate," to use Kenneth Burke's Latinate pun)
between the elements that comprise a contradiction. Normally later eighteenth-century poets avoided those strategies
by which the poet presents his awareness of opposites
working within. In other words, Empson's seventh type of
ambiguity, "that of full contradiction, marking a division in
the author's mind,"[22] is least congenial to these poets.
Empson calls this type "the most ambiguous that can be
conceived" because, I presume, it is the type that risks the
most in two different ways: (1) it is the type likely to give us
the most intimate information about the poet; (2) it is the
type that most threatens the integrity of the poem.

For the first point, it is precisely this kind of information that the poets of the later eighteenth century did not want us to have, even though we can find a number of critical statements where the opposite observation seems to be made. For example, late in the century Alexander Knox wrote that the greater the poet's ability "in expressing what he himself feels so as to make others participate in his feelings, the more, undoubtedly, does he possess of the radical qualities of a poet."[23] What Knox meant, however, is that the specific genius of the poet is implicit in the way he taps the universe of feeling; he renders feeling in "ideal pictures," each of which is an aspect of the total feeling viewed not dialectically but complementarily.

For the second point, one should not forget that the ambiguity of full contradiction is a type most at home in metaphysical poetry. Ian Jack's observation is very telling here:

[the] satirical tendency implicit in Metaphysical poetry from the first is very marked in the work of Cleveland; in Butler, it might be said, this tendency becomes fully developed. . . . More brilliantly than any previous poet, he [Butler] used [metaphysical] "wit" for the purposes of low satire. . . . *Hudibras* was one of the principal channels by which the "wit" of the earlier part of the century was transmitted to the greatest of the Augustans.[24]

Thus the Augustans could be at ease with metaphysical wit *after* they had converted it into Augustan wit. The satiric victim is the person who, as in Dryden's and Pope's satires, emerges as guilty of metaphysical wit; he contains opposites within himself. The satirist shows us how it appears to be and to behave in this way, and when Johnson spoke against Cowley he was of course arguing against the perversion of a typical feeling easily shared by others.

One way in which a typical feeling can be shared by others is to render it typologically and endow it with the embellishments of iconography. Emotions thus become objects of contemplation and are deprived of their compulsions; they become actors rather than enactments. The poet arranges the ways in which the emotion is to be seen by the reader. Wordsworth and Coleridge, however, tend rather to concentrate upon the refractoriness of emotions, and they frequently suggest a bifurcation between the conscious intentions of character and the obstinacy of emotions released from their hiding places within.

Frye remarks that "pity without an object has never to my knowledge been given a name."[25] But it has; its name is sentimentality, a state of mind which exists in perpetual readiness of response. Sentimental people all conform to this condition: a state of emotional receptivity or vulnerability, a disposition to weep. "The Castaway" is a product of this state of mind trying to locate its proper object, an attempt to explain the poet's emotion by fastening it upon a situation relevant to his own but different if not less grievous. Romantic poetry is sometimes spoken about as though the poet desired to be rid of the object, absorb it into himself through his omnivorous capacity to devour all that is not himself. But the opposite proposition is at least equally true. Part of the job was to reinstate the object, making it a symbolic rather than an analogical fact of experience as Cowper did in "The Castaway." Wordsworth went to low characters or innocents because he thought of the kind of action described here as elemental and thus more forcibly affective within minds of less sophistication. The use of an "old nurse" or "monk" or "parish clerk" which Jeffrey recommended to give "grace" to a narration is very much like using the object to give *point* to it.[26]

In both cases the poet deals in properties. Some poets, like Donne, can do this very effectively, but normally only where there is extraordinary license to bring these properties to bear upon each other through some such agency as wit. Without such an agency the representation of feeling, as in much of Collins and Gray, is likely to seem remote and impersonal.[27] Here again Romantic subtlety is largely a matter of trusting to unlikely sources, of experimenting with what seemed to many early nineteenth-century reviewers accidental characteristics and low characters in the hope that the seemingly peripheral would define a new center of, and for, consciousness. Considered in terms of the representation of states of mind, and in terms of those unanticipated evocations of which I have spoken before, this is what did happen. It is a large part of what a shift of sensibility is all about.

But it is by no means all. It signifies the poet's concern with the probable image but does not clearly define the conjunction of the probable and the marvelous. To this subject we can now begin to be attentive, and it is with Wordsworth's lyric poetry between the publication of the *Lyrical Ballads* in 1798 and the *Poems in Two Volumes* of 1807 that we will be chiefly occupied.

As early as 1798, in the advertisement to the *Lyrical Ballads,* Wordsworth requests his readers to ask themselves if his poetry "contains a natural delineation of human passions, human characters, and human incidents." When he later comes to distinguish between fancy and imagination, the latter is associated with inevitability, the former with accident or caprice. Moreover, "Fancy depends upon the rapidity and profusion with which she scatters her thoughts and images," and in a note to "The Thorn," fancy is "the power by which pleasure and surprise are excited by sudden varieties of situation and an accumulated imagery." To Wordsworth, fancy is very much what it was to Dryden, the image-making faculty of the mind, independent of judgment, and therefore given to forming playful or far-fetched similitudes. On the other hand, imagination is associated with "unity," with the "eternal," with "certain fixed laws," and, in two different places within the Preface of 1815, with "properties" that are "inherent" and therefore "internal."[28]

Wordsworth illustrates the play of fancy by reference to Cotton's "Ode upon Winter." He refers to the "most lively description of the entrance of Winter, with his retinue, as 'A palsied king,' and yet a military monarch,—advancing for conquest with his army; the several bodies of which, and their arms and equipments, are described with a rapidity of detail, and a profusion of *fanciful* comparisons, which indicate on the part of the poet extreme activity of intellect, and a corresponding hurry of delightful feeling."[29] Yet fancy is arbitrary and does not deal in the essential. In "To the Same Flower," the seventh poem under "Poems of the Fancy," Wordsworth writes:

> Oft on the dappled turf at ease
> I sit, and play with similes,
> Loose types of things through all degrees,
>   Thoughts of thy raising:
> And many a fond and idle name
> I give to thee, for praise or blame,
> As is the humour of the game,
>   While I am gazing.

W. J. B. Owen remarks that the "image of Fancy is not inevitable, and . . . the poet is aware that it is not inevitable: alternative views of the subject, alternative attitudes of the poet towards his subject, are possible."[30] Imagination, however, orders relations in terms of inevitability; fancy orders merely in relation to the "loose types of things." Inevitability is a function of imitation. For example: "However exalted a notion we would wish to cherish of the character of a Poet, it is obvious, that while he describes and imitates passions, his employment is in some degree mechanical, compared with the freedom and power of real and substantial action and suffering."[31] To imitate "real and substantial action" is to be concerned with that which is of permanent interest to mankind. Moreover, man's inevitable interests, his permanent interests, are related to his most enduring and most basic identity, that of the rustic. In a letter to Southey, prefacing *Peter Bell,* Wordsworth explained that the poem "was composed under a belief that the Imagination not only does not require for its exercise the intervention of supernatural agency, but that, though such agency be excluded, the faculty may be called forth as imperiously, and for kindred results of pleasure, *by incidents within the compass of poetic probability,* in the humblest departments of daily life"[32] (italics mine).

He specifically rejects any rhetorical device to elevate the language of his poetry. He speaks of using "a plainer and more emphatic language," but then adds that this language has been "purified . . . from . . . its real defects." Nevertheless, such a language, even prior to purification, is one "arising out of repeated experience and regular feelings," and is "a more permanent . . . language." The reference to "repeated experience" and "regular feelings" suggests a distinction between the familiar and salubrious on the one hand and the unique and abnormal on the other. He cautions his reader that the real language of men arises from normative experience. He thus defines language as an expression of a particular kind of character, that best and most enduring type of man, from whose language, or a selection thereof, the best style derives. The purer the feelings expressed, the more enduring will be the language in which feeling finds expression: "the affecting parts of Chaucer are almost always expressed in language pure and universally intelligible even to this day." Where Dryden had spoken of rhyme as a medium proportioned to the events represented by the tragic dramatist, Wordsworth has in view a language proportioned to the permanent interests and permanent identity of man. Later this language and the imagination are brought into relation: "in works of *imagination* and *sentiment* . . . they require and exact one and the same language."[33]

Yet, language is very problematical for Wordsworth, and he virtually abandons his literal insistence upon the rustic's diction for something else, "composing accurately in the spirit of such selection." He says that this "amounts to the same thing" as "selecting from the real language of men," but it does not. Wordsworth's distrust of poetic diction, the diction he notoriously associates with Gray's "Sonnet [on the Death of Mr Richard West]," springs from his distrust of poetry viewed as something adventitious, distinct from the experience of most men at most times, distinct at least from that which is most important, inevitable, and permanent to human interests. We may see, however, that it was Wordsworth's intention, seldom credited by the reviewers, to introduce a new kind of public poetry because he felt that the exaggerated poetry of the fancy was disintegrating and uninevitable, in brief, a poetry in which man was not writing to men. The polemical character of the prose writings suggests strongly his conviction that poetry had ceased to be a proper moral instrument, and to view his own poetry in these terms is to recognize his revolution as a reformation. It is thus that he remarks: "there are few persons of good sense, who would not allow that the dramatic parts of composition are defective, in proportion as they deviate from the real language of nature, and are coloured by a diction of the Poet's own, either peculiar to him as an individual Poet or belonging simply to Poets in general."[34]

We return therefore to imitation. The mimetic basis of Wordsworth's art is Aristotelian and dramatic.[35] Its most typical lyric mode is elegiac because the action Wordsworth most characteristically imitates is the recognition and assimilation of loss. This is his "real and substantial action and suffering." As in a tragedy, character suffers a recognition, suffers a gain in consciousness or growth of the mind, suffers the transmutation of loss into gain, suffers further the understanding that loss and gain are inseparable.

As with Blake's poetry, Wordsworth's is commonly concerned with innocence and experience as states of the soul, and the meaning Wordsworth implicitly attaches to both states approximates Blake's own definitions. Several of the poems from the 1807 edition are as much songs of the innocent state as anything written by Blake. A partial listing would include, "To a Butterfly," "The Green Linnet," "To a Young Lady," "The Sparrow's Nest," and "Written in March." The last, subsequently enlisted under "Poems of the Imagination," reads very much like Blake's "Spring" of *Innocence:*

> The cock is crowing,
> The stream is flowing,
> The small birds twitter,
> The lake doth glitter,
> The green field sleeps in the sun;
> The oldest and youngest
> Are at work with the strongest;
> The cattle are grazing,
> Their heads never raising;
> There are forty feeding like one!

"To a Butterfly" and "To the Cuckoo" are poems equally reminiscent of *Innocence* and resemble in their reflective and nostalgic tone Blake's "The Ecchoing Green." Others such as "The Small Celandine" and "A Complaint" are songs of the contrary state, and the latter poem in particular could be profitably compared with "The Angel" of Blake's *Experience.* Below is "A Complaint" in its entirety:

> There is a change—and I am poor;
> Your Love hath been, nor long ago,
> A Fountain at my fond Heart's door,

Whose only business was to flow;
And flow it did; not taking heed
Of its own bounty, or my need.
What happy moments did I count!
Bless'd was I then all bliss above!
Now, for this consecrated Fount
Of murmuring, sparkling, living love,
What have I? shall I dare to tell?
A comfortless, and hidden Well.

A well of love—it may be deep—
I trust it is, and never dry:
What matter? if the Waters sleep
In silence and obscurity.
—Such change, and at the very door
Of my fond Heart, hath made me poor.

Mark Reed notes that the earliest surviving evidence of Wordsworth's awareness of Blake's work is probably the period "between Feb 12 and Aug 25, esp. between mid-Mar and mid-Apr, or May 8 and June 10" of 1807.[36] During this period William and Mary copied several songs from *Innocence* and *Experience* into the Commonplace Book, but since *Poems in Two Volumes* was published on May 8 of that year it seems unlikely that any of the songs in this collection were influenced by Blake.

We need not posit any Blakean influence, for at least as early as 1798 Wordsworth was writing poems of innocence and experience. As a state of the soul, innocence exists prior to the consciousness of death ("We are Seven"). It therefore implies the indefinite duration in time of values and beliefs that have remained successfully unchallenged. The best examples of the dawning state of experience in Wordsworth's early poetry are undoubtedly offered by the Lucy poems, begun during Dorothy and William's stay at Goslar in the closing years of the century. Four of them end with the recognition of Lucy's death, the fifth, which Moorman suggests may have been the first composed, "Strange fits of passion," ends with the fear that Lucy may be dead. Wordsworth never published them as a group; three were later included in "Poems Founded on the Affections" and two in "Poems of the Imagination."

Since there appears to be no reason to consider the poems in any particular order, let me begin with "I travelled among unknown men." The poet speaks of England, about the love he bears for a place, and yet the poem is about Lucy. Initially we have a curious situation and a curious formula: the poet departs from England to learn what it is he loves but returns to tell us of the loss of Lucy. It perhaps does not make any difference whether Lucy died before he left England or after he returned; in any event the poem does not tell us. The formula is: departure–discovery–return–loss. What seems important to the poem is not Lucy, but England, for in the four-stanza poem she does not make an appearance until it is more than half over. Further, England's presence is dominant in a number of ways: we hear of England's "shore," England's "mountains," a "fire" that is English, along with "mornings," "nights," "bowers," and that "last green field." Emerging late in the poem is Lucy, an unselfconscious object performing simple actions. She "turned" her wheel, "played" in the bowers, and "surveyed" a field. Yet the poem strongly suggests that England is more dear because she contributed her presence to English objects, and, if this is so, in another way England gains because Lucy is presumably *in* a last green English field. The poet's awareness of England is deepened by his awareness of Lucy's death, and England is more dear both for what England and the poet have lost.

Moreover we have the somewhat curious situation of a solitary poet reflecting on the solitary Lucy. He "travelled among unknown men"; Lucy's activities, such as they are, are carried on without the intrusion of another presence. We do not know the precise meaning of "till then" in stanza one even after we have read the poem. Does it mean that he did not know what love he bore to England until he left England? Or can it mean that until Lucy's death he could not gauge and measure his love for England? The meaning of "melancholy dream" can be inferred from Wordsworth's biography, and the phrase traced to his earlier trust in the French Revolution. Yet, in the midst of much uncertain information, we hear of "love," "joy," "desire," and "cherished," a richness of emotion existent in a context of imprecise reference.

He has travelled, discovered, and resolved. She has done nothing that is not spontaneous or, we might almost say, involuntary. He has built up a painfully achieved certainty of values, while Lucy has built nothing and has no recorded consciousness in the poem. But the greatest difference between the poet and Lucy is that his solitariness was not sufficient; everything in the work leads us to believe that hers was. The separation between Lucy and poet seems focused therefore on his prior restlessness and on her solitary condition of simple stasis. Thus, in the context of the poem, her death *seems* a far less complex change than the poet's change from restless travel, perplexed by a "melancholy dream," to his return to England.

And if it is less complex the reason may be found in another of these songs. Lucy changes from turning her wheel to being turned: "Rolled round in earth's diurnal course." The difference between a being *in* nature and her nonbeing *of* nature, however painful to the speaker, minimizes the separation from life that Lucy endures. In other words, Lucy's identity, beyond self-consciousness, is beyond change; her innocence is not destroyed by death but confirmed by it, and, as the second stanza of the poem tells us, "she" continues to exert a presence though it is without "motion" or "force." Both qualities have been usurped, absorbed or assimilated, into that greater motion of which she has always been a part.

To return therefore to "I travelled among unknown men," we may recognize that against Lucy's eternal rightness has been set the poet's stir and fretfulness. What at first reading seems the major difference in the poem—that between Lucy alive and Lucy dead—is a major difference only to the poet, but that it is so to him defines a consciousness to be compared and contrasted with Lucy's. That she has been absorbed into that green field with which her humanness was already in perfect intimacy points to a state of the soul that time and mortality cannot alter. Lucy's eternal rightness is innocence invulnerable.

In these elegiac poems death leaves a legacy of quiet wonder to the survivor, a kind of still place in the landscape of the mind, a momentary repose of the active consciousness. In "Three years she grew in sun and shower," Lucy's death leaves a "calm, and quiet scene," a temporary equilibrium, a pause between "what has been, / And never more will be." In the stillness shared by the heath and the observer, nature and man come together, but not in the mood of sentimental reflection. The eternal living nature meets with the eternal fact of mortality in the silence beyond mere commentary, beyond mere eulogy, only to be punctuated by objects, by "heath," by "rocks, and stones, and trees." Into such objects, as they register upon the mind, slip the intimations of experience, of separation and distance, of thoughts that will soon come to lie "too deep for tears."

At first glance the penultimate line of "A slumber did my spirit seal" may strike us as odd. The rather recondite, scientific term "diurnal" seems out of place. But its impersonal descriptiveness underscores the flat monosyllables of the last line. The relation between "diurnal" and "rocks, and stones, and trees" is similar to that between the last and the penultimate lines of "She dwelt among the untrodden ways": "But she is in her grave, and, oh, / The difference to me!" The last line states a difference without definition, except as "difference" is different from all the monosyllables preceding it. It is not "grave" that makes the difference but "difference" itself, and the two words in juxtaposition call attention not only to Lucy's death but to the effect of that death as it registers upon the mind of the poet and alters reality for him. In this early poetry, in particular, we tend to receive from Wordsworth a poetry highly resistant to definition yet clearly significant of changes that have occurred within the speaker, changes that are momentous and cannot be undone, of a wholeness that has been lost and "never more will be." In one sense the Lucy poems are poems of Wordsworth's own descent into the conditions of experience, poems of the recognition of sunderings and fractures, of grief that cannot be outlived, of knowledge given that can never be forgotten.

After all that has been said it is almost impertinent to ask, of what did Lucy die? Perhaps the best answer is that she died so that Wordsworth the elegiac poet could be born. He virtually says as much in the poem we have been considering. "A slumber did my spirit seal" is an image; it means obviously that his awareness of death was sealed off from his consciousness. But Lucy's death is sealed by the slumber of the grave. The poet's slumber was a living slumber; Lucy's death is a dying slumber. The initial image drives toward its odd counterpart. The poem opens distances between poet and Lucy and closes those distances. Lucy's death is a kind of benefit; it awakens him to terrible knowledge. Her sleep is his wakefulness, whereas she waked in his slumber. Between seeming ("she seemed a thing") and knowing (waking) lies the distance between innocence and experience.

Finally it is the shock of recognition that is the subject of these poems, as "Strange fits of passion" also makes clear. As with Blake, passion is the vehicle of experience and love is the agent of self-knowledge. The "fond and wayward" thoughts that "slide / Into a Lover's head" are the unexpected and unwelcome truths of man's mortality.

In "To M. H." the challenge of experience does not arise; it is a love poem complete and unviolated by the intrusion of loss, and nature lends herself to the illusion of the "sweet dream." As such it is an epithalamion, a song of the wedding between Mary and William, but Mary transfigured by the poet into nature, nature receptive and dowering the poet's imagination. Human identity and natural forms merge to become one form, one identity, even as in "There was a Boy," the first of the poems Wordsworth grouped under "Poems of the Imagination." The youth in his "silence" is informed by "the voice / Of mountain-torrents," by "the visible scene" entering "unawares into his mind," by all the "solemn imagery" of "rocks" and "woods" and that "uncertain heaven received / Into the bosom of the steady lake." Nature and its objects take possession of the boy as by a gift of grace, answering the unconscious prayer of "hands / Pressed closely palm to palm." As in the Lucy poems, nature takes its own, and the speaker stands "mute" over the boy's grave, echoing the earlier informing "silence" of the youth. Innocence is the gift that is given and taken; experience is the legacy, the diminished thing that descends from the glory and the dream. It is only one of the many occasions in Wordsworth's early poetry of that which "never more will be."

Man is whole and in harmony with himself, Wordsworth had said in the 1800 Preface, when his passions and manners are "incorporated with the beautiful and permanent forms of nature."[37] The prescription is more Blakean than has been generally suspected, another version of the unfallen world, of innocence, of complete containment and contentment within a joyfully animated nature. But whereas Blake knows it will not endure, Wordsworth hopes to graft it onto time, and the inevitable result is a poetry of loss, of elegiac lament. Strategies of permanence contribute heavily to the importance of recovery in the Wordsworthian lyric. The "emotion recollected in tranquillity," the locus classicus of recoverable feeling embodied in the conception of "spots of time," defines the conservative bias of Wordsworth's imagination. The effort to return, to discover the precise moment when feelings have been created and first recognized, is the continuing burden of *The Prelude*. In book two Wordsworth muses on the place he had known as a child and speaks of his later return to discover that a "smart Assembly-room . . . perk'd and flar'd" where once there was "A grey stone / Of native rock." The experience imposes upon him a sense of discontinuity, of containing "Two consciousnesses, conscious of myself / And of some other Being" (2: 32). The discovery is unsettling, the spot violated. Time and place are islands in the flow of being. Thus Wordsworth talks of "the soul / Remembering how she felt, but what she felt / Remembering not" (2: 334–36). The imagination builds its own traditions from the stored and recoverable sensations that are the basis of a "creative sensibility" (2: 379). Thus the poet is prophet of conservative man, of the rustic who does not break faith with time, whose identity is "incorporated with the beautiful and permanent forms of nature." But the faith is always, or almost always, broken, and between the hope of what will be and the recognition of what is, Wordsworth's poetry moves. Over and again Wordsworth tells the story of this fall. It is the drama of "The Brothers" and of "Michael," of Michael whose "blind love" is "the pleasure which there is in life itself," and of his son: "exceeding was the love he bare to him." To bind the one love to the other is the burden of Michael's life, to commemorate and to transmit "the life thy Fathers lived, / Who, being innocent, did for that cause / Bestir them in good deeds."

For Thomas Gray time had been the vehicle of loss; Wordsworth's position is more ambivalent, hence more complex. Time is invested with moments of sensation that save us from our present selves: "oft, in lonely rooms" the restorative effects of fidelity conserved, stored up, rescue us from the vacuity of the present. But time is equally the vehicle of loss, the medium in which we betray our imperfect devotion. Blake deals with a similar conception by transmuting the tragic knowledge of a sundered harmony, the fall from innocence, into the potentially revolutionary conditions engendered by experience. To fall, then, is to rise more greatly, and the process leads to the state of the fully awakened imagination characteristic of the prophetic poet. In effect this is to say that Blake's conception of experience is informed by the necessity for mental warfare: the false forms of the fallen world call forth the poet, and will always call him forth no matter what the changing character of those false forms. The Fall then is a continually recurrent fact of human life, almost oddly desirable because when such conditions no longer pertain, imagination, having no longer a purpose, will cease to exist.

Wordsworth's conception is very different and comes to limit his growth as a poet. Like Blake, he understands experience as an internal fact, something both probable and marvelous, a part of the human condition so intrinsic to human identity that it cannot be eradicated. Yet throughout the very early poems, Wordsworth seeks ways to minimize its reality, to limit and curtail its effects by strategies that begin with recovery and lead to transcendence. To begin with sensation is to end by shedding it, to escape from the husk of reality and "become a living soul." From a Blakean point of view such strategies are tricks of the mind, founded upon nostalgia for values locked in the past and only inconsistently available. Another way of making the same observation, from a putatively Blakean perspective, is to regard innocence as a recurrent temptation. It is a little like the situation in which Thel finds herself. To return to the vales of Har and Heva is to return to an innocence that gradually gives way to sterile senility, a collapse of the mind inward upon itself through fear and loss of faith. This is why Blake sees in Wordsworth "the Natural Man rising up against the Spiritual Man Continually."[38] But because in Wordsworth the natural man is the basis of the spiritual man, and because Wordsworth's ideal man is the rustic, he keeps returning to and mining the sources of fidelity he finds there. Natural man, however, is only imperfectly the spiritual man, and the violation of the legacy of fidelity is the sin to which the flesh is heir.

Thus Luke breaks the trust. Thus Leonard, in "The Brothers," leaves forever the place in which James (the brother whose death is the consequence of a broken covenant) has died, for the placelessness of ocean. Thus the world rushes in, necessitating the rebuilding of the ideal over and again; hence the summoning of the monkish figure of the hermit who "by his fire" is natural man illuminated by the grace of sustained fidelity, "blind love." Much the same observation may be made of that larger and bleaker figure, the Leech-gatherer of "Resolution and Independence." Admonishing like a heaven-descended emissary, "like a man from some far region sent," he is transformed by the poet into emblems of permanence, into "huge stone" and "seabeast." Like Michael he has endured the discipline of the spirit that nature imposes, surviving as an example of

> How exquisitely the individual Mind
> (And the progressive powers perhaps no less
> Of the whole species) to the external World
> Is fitted,—& how exquisitely too,
> Theme this but little heard of among Men
> The external World is fitted to the Mind.

To which Blake replied, "You shall not bring me down to believe such fitting and fitted I know better & Please your Lordship." Yet such is the myth central to Wordsworth's poetry; his archetypal figure is the post-Edenic Adam, the rustic whose "covenant," as Geoffrey Hartman puts it, "of mind and nature, the marriage of heaven and earth," is, as Hartman later admits, "mainly a hope, and faith, and desire."[39]

The convenant is made to be broken; its breaking is to be suffered, to be reestablished, to be broken again. It is formed in innocence, lost in the initial oncoming of experience, deepened in the widening human sympathy that is the ultimate achievement of experience. The Fall is into our common humanity, into the "philosophic mind." In the recesses of a green wood the hermit of "Tintern Abbey" inhabits his cave. The imagination has in summoning him created the momentary monument to its own hopes, to the "sublime . . . [and] blessed mood" which is the product of reintegrating man and nature. Contrapuntally, however, there sounds the "still, sad music of humanity" having the "power / To chasten and subdue." The elegiac note comes through and grows. The marriage of man and nature is not to be a simple joyous event but a discipline of the spirit.

Unlike Blake, Wordsworth does not do battle with the stern conception of morality that haunts his poetry. The world conceived as a place of moral imperative grows within his work, necessitating by 1802 the creation of the gravely reproving Leech-gatherer whose speech was "like a stream / Scarce heard; nor word from word could I divide." The "stream" is sustaining faith issuing from the uncorrupted heart, what Wordsworth was later to call "conscience . . . God's most intimate presence in the soul, / And his most perfect image in the World." It is interesting to note, however, that "Resolution and Independence" was written (in its

initial form) in the first week of May 1802, after Wordsworth
had begun, but not finished, the "Intimations Ode." The
latter follows upon the flush of lyric poetry in the years
1798–1802 and explores as the early elegiac poems do not
the wisdom lying within elegiac recognitions. Here, more
than anywhere else, Wordsworth elaborates his version of
the Fortunate Fall.

Only the first four stanzas of the poem were written in
1802, and two years were to pass before Wordsworth returned to it and completed it. The vitality of this great poem
depends upon the interplay between ideas of innocence and
experience, and the special question posed by the "Ode" is
what can be done with a diminished thing? What is given
initially to the child of the "Ode" is the "primal sympathy." It
is responsible for the "visionary gleam," for "the glory and
the dream." Further, the primal sympathy legitimizes the
several offices the child holds: he is "Nature's Priest," "best
Philosopher," "Eye among the blind," "Mighty Prophet,"
and "Seer blest." Such offices are not merely honorific; they
are certified by the primal sympathy which is the guarantor
of all such high functions, functions which, while not illusory,
are transitory.

Wordsworth's conception of Earth in the poem is something akin to Blake's idea of Nature in "The Mental Traveller."[40] Earth is a stepmother, man her "Inmate":

> The homely Nurse doth all she can,
> To make her Foster-child, her Inmate Man,
> Forget the glories he hath known,
> And that imperial palace whence he came.

Unlike the old woman of Blake's poem, Wordsworth's Earth
is not a viciously delusory reality but a somewhat hapless
figure offering comforts of a second-rate kind, but with "no
unworthy aim." Like many of Wordsworth's poems the
"Ode" is about someone growing up, or growing away, or,

better yet, about growing down, which is to say that growth is diminution of power. It is a common paradoxical theme of his poetry, and Wordsworth had engaged the subject in "Resolution and Independence": poets who begin in "gladness" end in "madness." In the "Ode" the child literally comes down, for "The Soul that rises with us, our life's Star, / Hath had elsewhere it's setting." Thus one of the leading questions is what good is grace given, when, as it would seem, human life progressively denies the efficacy of the gift? It is a Miltonic question.

Wordsworth's answer lies in the recognition that what is suffered is the transmutation of the gift, the primal sympathy, into its human form, which is wisdom. The growing down, the fall from celestial comity, is accompanied by a grace that seems initially merely a cruel remembrance. Yet from another perspective, that of man as Earth's inmate, the gift sustains us in our fall into common nature, making possible our growth into the fullness of human nature. Two metaphors of travel contain the conception within which Wordsworth's vision is apparent. The child descends into the condition of man; this is the descent from innocence and appears as pure loss. From within the conditions of experience the man travels "farther from the East"; that is, "inland" or toward death. This is the second stage of the journey into common nature, away from the light or the sun or all those various illuminations of the glory that is past or passing. Yet the journey toward death is also necessarily a journey into the completeness of the human condition, and as such it is a journey having as its goal the knowledge of the "human heart by which we live."

Because of this second progress, conducted in fidelity to the primal sympathy, the faithful observance of "an eye / That hath kept watch o'er man's mortality," the gift, the "something given," irradiates the journey toward death. This is the wisdom of elegy transposed into the key of Wordsworth's humanism vitalized by the sympathetic imagination. To come full circle, then, what is suffered is wisdom; the Fall is into the "still, sad music of humanity" heard in "Tintern Abbey," into the "sober colouring" seen in the "Intimations Ode." It is the burden of man in experience, articulated by the poet but carried by all men in those "thoughts that do often lie too deep for tears." Finally it is Wordsworth's "truth, not individual and local, but general, and operative; not standing upon external testimony, but carried alive into the heart by passion."[41]

Though the list is by no means intended to be exhaustive, the word *innocence* commonly appears in Wordsworth's early poems. It occurs in "To a Highland Girl," "Michael," "The sun has long been set," "Who fancied what a pretty sight," "The Blind Highland Boy," the "Intimations Ode," "Ruth," "The Dungeon," "The Affliction of Margaret," and "Repentance." Of these poems, "To a Highland Girl," "The sun has long been set," "Who fancied what a pretty sight," and "The Blind Highland Boy," are poems of the innocent state, the last very much in the spirit of Blake's "Little Boy Lost" and "Little Boy Found." Not all of Wordsworth's poems definitive of the state of innocence employ the term, but those that do specify a state of genial receptivity to the harmonious conditions of the natural world perfectly in keeping with other poems from the 1807 volumes mentioned earlier and with the "Anecdote for Fathers" and "We are Seven."

Characteristically, though not invariably, innocence is associated with childhood or youth. On occasion Wordsworth hopes that innocence will persist into age (as in "To a Highland Girl" and in his prayer for Dorothy in "Tintern Abbey"). Other pieces employing the word *innocence,* such as "Michael," the "Intimations Ode," "Ruth," "The Dungeon," "The Affliction of Margaret," and "Repentance," are all poems about the loss of innocence and the oncoming of experience. In many of these, prison references or prison imagery are conspicuous. Such is the case in "Ruth," "The Dungeon," "The Forsaken," the "Intimations Ode," "The Convict," and "The Affliction of Margaret." The state of experience is commonly associated not only with confinement but with loss of vision. In the poems of experience— "Tintern Abbey," the "Intimations Ode," "Resolution and Independence"—references to "blind" are frequent; and on at least one other occasion in the early poems—in "There was a Boy"—experience is identified with another form of impaired sensation, muteness.

Again, not all the poems of experience use such imagery, but it is striking how often prison imagery and blindness (or muteness) define a pattern of reference by which Wordsworth controls the poems of experience. In "Tintern Abbey" the "beauteous forms" have not been "as is a landscape to a blind man's eye." The poet of "Resolution and Independence" is victimized by "blind thoughts," and in the "Ode" the child is an "eye among the blind." In "The Blind Highland Boy," a poem of the innocent state, the boy is narrowly rescued from the "perilous deep" and restored to the protective guardianship of the loving mother.

Often the characters of whom Wordsworth approves tend to be good readers, therefore not blind. Michael's mind is "like a book," the Leech-gatherer "conned" the muddy water, "as if he had been reading in a book." The child of the "Intimations Ode" "read'st the eternal deep." Those who survive the conditions of experience do so because they are good readers, and in fact need to be good readers, since experience is associated with diminished primary vision and the growth, as it were, of secondary vision, of reading. Experience is also frequently identified with the betrayal of personal fidelity, and many of the early poems deal with the literal fact of desertion. To survive within experience requires that the mind be well stored: Dorothy's mind "shall be as a mansion for all lovely forms." The spots of time theory is nothing less than a repository of such moments and such forms. The mind must be capable of fidelity, the familiar expression of which is human sympathy, but also capable of duty—another, more stern form of fidelity.

A definition of experience arises implicitly from the major lyrics. The problem is to preserve that residue of grace which permits seeing. Thus in "Resolution and Independence" there is "peculiar grace, / A leading from above, a something given." In the "Ode" the something given is "primal sympathy," convertible to human sympathy, from "eye" to "heart." In "To a Highland Girl" "grace / Hath led me to this lonely place." The place is a spot: "In spots like these it is we prize / Our Memory, feel that she hath eyes." Memory is itself a reader. As we grow older we read with the heart (the speaker of "To a Highland Girl" is "pleased at heart"), or, as in "Tintern Abbey," Wordsworth reads in another "the language of my former heart." To move from eye to heart is almost definitive of the movement from innocence to experience when such a transition is informed with saving grace. The context is religious, the natural man informed by the spiritual man. As in the "Ode," "sober colouring" is the dilution that survives, what remains if we are faithful to the conditions of our common mortality.

The resolution is far from Blakean, but the terms of innocence and experience are comparable, the problem of the fall into common humanity the same. Wordsworth's resolutions are knowledge, duty, discipline, the human heart, stored and shared forms, the residue of grace. Blake's, in a word, is imagination, the persistence of Christ reborn and triumphant. Wordsworth's resolution suggests Christ as Man of Sorrows, humanized as elegiac prophet, interpreter of elegiac experience.

All of the poems to which I have been making reference

were composed no later than 1804–1806. They bring
Wordsworth up to the time when the greater part of the
Prelude was to be written and *The Excursion* begun in earnest.
They define the prevailing character of the work done in the
years 1798–1806, and they mark the major period of his
lyric poetry.

Like Blake, Wordsworth is a religious poet, to the extent at
least that he seeks the probable image of man in the fact of his
fall from "primal sympathy" and finds in the fidelity that yet
remains the motive for spiritual discipline.[42] Yet to speak of
Wordsworth as a religious poet raises certain problems.
Moorman rightly observes similarities between the last hundred lines of the fifth book of the *Prelude* and the "Intimations
Ode." Each was written in the late winter or early spring of
1804. For example, from the *Prelude*:

> our childhood sits,
> Our simple childhood sits upon a throne
> That hath more power than all the elements. (531–33)

> The time of trial, ere we learn to live
> In reconcilement with our stinted powers,
> To endure this state of meagre vassalage;
> Unwilling to forego, confess, submit,
> Uneasy and unsettled; yoke-fellows
> To custom, mettlesome, and not yet tam'd
> And humbled down. . . .   (540–46)

> A tract of the same isthmus which we cross
> In progress from our native continent
> To earth and human life: I mean to speak
> Of that delightful time of growing youth
> When cravings for the marvellous relent,
> And we begin to love what we have seen;
> And sober truth, experience, sympathy,
> Take stronger hold of us. . . .   (560–67)

> I am sad
> At thought of raptures now for ever flown,
> Even unto tears. . . .   (568–70)

That wish for something loftier, more adorn'd,
Than is the common aspect, daily garb
Of human life.   (599–601)

In the fourth book of *The Excursion,* written somewhat
more than two years later, Wordsworth resumes the language of the "Ode" and book five of the *Prelude,* but the
differences are so substantial that they require further consideration. Like the speaker of the "Ode," the Wanderer notices
that "powers depart" but that as children the

> dread source,
> Prime, self-existing, cause and end of all . . .
>   . . . didst wrap the cloud
> Of infancy around us, that thyself
> Therein, with our simplicity awhile
> Might'st hold, on earth, communion undisturbed. . . .
>   (79–80, 83–86)

> Still, it may be allowed me to remember
> What visionary powers of eye and soul
> In youth were mine. . . .   (110–12)

> The measure of my soul was filled with bliss,
> And holiest love; as earth, sea, air, with light,
> With pomp, with glory, with magnificence!
>   (120–22)

> Those fervent raptures are for ever flown. . . . (123)

What next occurs is very different from the resolutions
explicit in both the "Ode" and the fifth book of the *Prelude.*
The disaffection brought about by the loss of visionary
power now resembles a moral failing, an excess, as the Wanderer calls it:

> the innocent Sufferer often sees
> Too clearly; feels too vividly; and longs
> To realize the vision, with intense
> And over-constant yearning;—there—there lies
> The excess, by which the balance is destroyed.
>   (174–78)

In the Wanderer's acknowledgement that "the endowment of immortal power / Is matched unequally with custom, time" (205–6), we are back again within the ambience of the "Ode," but by way of consolation what lies within man are "helps,"

> Vigils of contemplation; praise; and prayer—
> A stream, which, from the fountain of the heart
> Issuing, however feebly, nowhere flows
> Without access of unexpected strength.   (218–21)

And thus it is that the Wanderer counsels

>   entire submission to the law
> Of conscience—conscience reverenced and obeyed,
> As God's most intimate presence in the soul,
> And his most perfect image in the world. (224–27)

The resolution is different in kind from what is offered in the "Ode"; a more specifically orthodox consolation is provided, one that had been growing in Wordsworth's poetry as early as the "Resolution and Independence" of 1802 but that now merged with the broader stream of Anglicanism. This tendency is not conspicuous in the 1807 edition of Wordsworth's poems, largely because many of the poems published there had been composed years earlier, and it is probably true that the death of John Wordsworth at sea in 1805 hastened William's turn to traditional Christian solace.

This is not at all to imply its total absence in earlier works but to suggest a growing Christian traditionalism in Wordsworth's poetry that was very marked by 1806. In an interesting letter written years later, in 1815, to Catherine Clarkson, Wordsworth answered the criticism brought against him by Parthenope Smith, one of Catherine's correspondents: "I have alluded to the Lady's errors of opinion. She talks of my being a worshiper of Nature. A passionate expression, uttered incautiously in the poem upon the Wye, has led her into this mistake; she, reading in cold-heartedness, and substituting the letter for the spirit. Unless I am greatly mistaken, there is nothing of this kind in *The Excursion*."[43] While not a repudiation of sentiments expressed in "Tintern Abbey," the letter strongly suggests the presence of more chastened, less "incautious" sentiments in *The Excursion*. But by 1806 the period of Wordsworth's major poetry was drawing to a close, a reflection which is justified by reference to dates of composition rather than publication.

The trials of experience are to be more largely rationalized within another framework, not that of the Christian humanism controlling the "Ode" but that of the more venerable theological teaching which it is the purpose of *The Excursion* to inculcate. To place Wordsworth exclusively within the context of Anglican thought is to minimize perilously the meanings that inform his engagement with elegy and to suggest too emphatically the religiously polemical character of that engagement.[44]

The recognitions that permeate his published poetry in the period 1798–1807 are by no means especially optimistic; in the *Poems in Two Volumes* innocence is deliberately courted, a nostalgic mood of the poet's mind that is finally violated by the great "Ode" itself. It represents Wordsworth's own triumph over the limitations he so acutely realized as implicit in experience. Having achieved that victory he was then enabled to build around it the solace of the traditional wisdom of Christianity, resignation to God's purposes, sustaining grace, the "helps" of conscience and duty, and Christian trust and humility. The "Ode" concludes one period of his work without prefiguring the renewed dedication explicit in the completed *Excursion* of 1814.

If in the poetry written after 1805 Wordsworth has been generally regarded as a less interesting poet than theretofore, the reason lies largely in the surrender of the intimate elegiac mode. And whatever the gain in theological clarity registered in *The Excursion,* the loss of his dramatic veracity, the decline in his power to delineate movingly and accurately the mind engaged with the contraries of innocence and experience is one of major proportions. Blake does not suffer this loss for two reasons. His confidence is never invested in the "natural" man, and, unlike Wordsworth, he recognizes experience as a delusion of the mind, nonetheless threatening for that reason but necessitating the militant vigilance of the imagination. Wordsworth moves toward a humbler and more modest conception of the mind's service and in so doing brings the greater period of his poetry to a conclusion, but not until he has recreated an image of human nature both probable and marvelous, the fusion of the ordinary and the sublime within the permanent image of man.

6
Conclusion

At the close of his seminal study *The Sublime,* Samuel Monk remarks: "As a general interpretation of the eighteenth century this study has probably nothing new to offer, but it has sought to show from its own point of view the slow and unconscious growth of English art away from the orderly garden of the Augustan age to the open fields (the jungle, if you will) of the romantic period."[1] A variation of Monk's modest disclaimer might with more reason be applied to this study. Much that has been offered in the way of discrete analysis will not be unfamiliar to students of eighteenth- and nineteenth-century poetry. Yet it is within the area of "general interpretation" that I suggest the usefulness of this work resides. Blake and Wordsworth are new poets summoned by old realities, responsive to the limits and limitations of their immediate predecessors and writing in reaction to them. The incorporation of the sublime within the subjective lyric I have taken to be one of their principal tasks, and the course of that activity has been charted. However, a further word needs to be said about the sublime. As a general topic it is much more than casually relevant to this inquiry. Consistently associated with religious experience, with the transporting image, with strong sensations, with the sympathetic imagination, and with exaltation and Shaftesburian rhapsody, the sublime appealed through the passions to man's enlarged awareness of himself as a being made in God's image, located in a universe informed by His presence.[2]

Angus Fletcher notices, for example, speaking especially of

Collins and Gray, that "the sublime poem does not in fact suggest the world of nature or of metaphor; it suggests ideal Shelleyan worlds—the enthusiasm for the ideal." We should, however, also bear in mind that the sublime offered an escape from the burden of a complex image of human nature, and the frequent association of the sublime with external phenomena, with mountains, deserts, and oceans, furthered an emphasis upon effect at the expense of analysis. John Gilbert Cooper, in 1755, taking as his text the line from *The Merchant of Venice,* "How sweet the Moonlight Sleeps upon that Bank!" stated: "That verb, taken from animal life, and transfer'd by the irresistible magic of poetry, to the before lifeless objects of the Creation, animates the whole scene, and conveys an instantaneous idea to the imagination what a solemn stillness is requir'd when the *peerless* Queen of Night is, in the full splendour of her majesty, thus lull'd to repose." To Abrams this "tendency to isolate a supremely poetic quality . . . and to locate this quality in the electrifying and transporting image or passage, rather than in the larger aspects of plot or design, is visible in all eighteenth-century critics who felt strongly the impact of Longinus."[3]

At the end of the century, Schiller offered an interesting analysis of the complex emotions attendant upon the sublime:

The feeling of the sublime is a mixed feeling. It is at once a painful state, which in its paroxysm is manifested in a kind of shudder, and a joyous state, that may rise to rapture, and which, without being properly a pleasure, is greatly preferred to every kind of pleasure by delicate souls. The union of two contrary sensations in one and the same feeling proves, in a peremptory manner, our moral independence. For as it is impossible that the same object should be with us in two opposite relations, so it follows that it is we *ourselves* who sustain two different relations with the object. It follows that these two opposed natures should be united in us, which, on the idea of this object, are brought into play in two perfectly opposed ways.[4]

To sustain complex feeling is undoubtedly a measure of enlarged capacity, and to this extent the sublime flattered while
appealing to the sensibilities of the reader. We have previously noticed how the descriptive ode of the middle years of
the century tended toward an affective structure, and we shall
again notice this subject in relation to Archibald Alison. A
succession of scenes, variously sublime, picturesque, or beautiful was strong matter for the sensibilities. Such a succession
offered a shifting and varied appeal to the passions and resulted in a poetry of rich emotive texture. But such a poetry,
finding its locus in sentiment, its justification in the idea that
the passions are the vehicles of self-exaltation, and hopefully
the instruments by which the ideal could be apprehended,
tended nevertheless to freight the mind with impressions and
images. Yet the ontology served by the transporting image
was undoubtedly a vital part of the sublime. To suggest that
the effect is greater than the immediately exciting cause implied that man is designed for a higher state of existence. The
feelings attendant upon the experience of sublimity offered
evidence for a primal spiritual unity, sundered by the Fall of
man but recoverable at least temporarily by the emotional
transport of the sublime.

Much of the effort of faculty psychology in the middle and
later years of the century was directed to justifying such
response, to arguing that enthusiasm was not a mere negation of the reason but something more like the direction of
the reason under the governance of inspiration. So Alexander
Gerard, one of the best of the mental mechanists, suggested:
"The fire of genius, like the divine impulse, raises the mind
above itself, and by the natural influence of imagination ac-
tuates it as if it were supernaturally inspired."[5] To speak
generally, the Augustan humanists enforced the truth of
human limitation consequent upon the Fall and ridiculed
over and again enthusiasm sanctioned by inner illumination.

To a very large extent the mid-century poets and critics reacted against the authority of this idea and against the poetry it sponsored.

In 1789 when Thomas Twining published his influential translation of the *Poetics,* to which he added "Two Dissertations on Poetical and Musical Imitation," he offered the view that the "description of passions and emotions by their sensible effects . . . [is what] principally deserves the name of *imitative.*"[6] To imitate in Twining's terms and to allegorize in Thomas Warton's were one and the same, and the proper poetic illustration of both views was found in Collins's delineations of Fear's "haggard eye" or Vengeance's "red Arm, expos'd and bare." For Blake and Wordsworth it was necessary to purge the sublime of its merely terrible effects and to bring it into relation with an enlarged conception of human purpose—that just and lively image of human nature about which English criticism had been speaking for well over a hundred years.

The more that one inquires into the eighteenth-century sublime, the more it reveals an oddity at its center: the attempt to repair, at one leap, a sundered spiritual unity and to restore directly and immediately the ideal that the soul seeks. Through certain forms, as Addison suggested in *Spectators* 411 to 415, art aided and contributed to this activity. Sacred poetry, *Paradise Lost* in particular, was the immediate literary locus for such values. Yet, as Paul Fussell reminds us, "Although the Augustan humanist values highly the Miltonic myths of human frailty and of both external and psychological hierarchy, his moral imagination luxuriates especially in recalling one particular scene. The humanist mind in the eighteenth century returns again and again to Book VIII of *Paradise Lost* and to the dialogue between Raphael and Adam about what we would call 'science'." However, when Addison came to consider *Paradise Lost* he remarked that Milton's "chief talent, and indeed his distinguishing excellence, lies in the sublimity of his thoughts"; it "is impossible for the Imagination of Man to distend itself with greater Ideas [i.e., images], than those which he has laid together in his first, second, and sixth Books."[7]

The distended imagination played an increasingly crucial role in the expectations of the eighteenth-century reader, particularly as the influence of the Augustan humanists declined in the middle and later years of the century. The effect of the distended imagination could be illustrated through the character of Satan, as Addison suggested in his discussion of the first two books of Milton's epic. Though in his view Milton's true hero remained intact, Satan's ruined divinity was the great supernatural fact, marvelous in itself, fearful as an example of God's omnipotence, and therefore a proper subject for the poet's sublime imagination. Yet any object vast and wonderful evoked feelings of sublimity. As William Duff said, the "sublime, in particular is the proper walk of a great Genius," and a "rude magnificence . . . throws the whole soul into a divine transport of admiration and amazement, which occupies and fills the mind, and at the same time inspires that solemn dread, that religious awe, which naturally results from the contemplation of the vast and wonderful." Daniel Webb commented in the same spirit: "The finest, and, at the same time, most pleasing sensations in nature, are those, which (if I may be allowed the expression) carry us out of ourselves, and bring us nearest to that divine original, from which we spring." Even Sir Joshua's sister, Frances Reynolds, was not immune: sublimity "is a pinnacle of beatitude, bordering upon horror, deformity, madness! an eminence from whence the mind, that dares to look farther, is lost!" It is as far as the imagination of man can carry, but it is the focus and center of everyman's imagination: "The idea of the supreme Being is, I imagine, in every breast, from the clown to the greatest philosopher, his point of sublimity!"[8] The hunger for the ideal found expression in the common formula: the soul of poetry is passion; great images are most capable of communicating passion to the reader; the highest expression of passion is sublimity.

Moreover, the sublime was viewed as a social instrument, a medium for the communication of the affections, the passionate tie that binds. Because language is a more effective instrument for the communication of emotions, it was usually a more highly regarded vehicle for the transmission of passion than was painting. Almost every critic who focused on the relation between the sister arts in the middle and later years of the century was attentive to this criterion and contended for the superiority of one art to the other on this basis. In his youthful *Enquiry* Burke observed: "The proper manner of conveying the *affections* of the mind from one to another, is by words." But it was generally agreed that, as Sir William Jones put it, "the finest parts of poetry, musick, and painting [in descending order of preference] are expressive of the *passions,* and operate on our minds by *sympathy*."[9]

To review critical attention to the sublime and the passions it sponsors is to perceive how traditionally conservative is Wordsworth's often cited remark that "poetry is the spontaneous overflow of powerful feelings." None of the literary associationists would have denied it; no critic tinged in the least by the emotionalism of the sublime would have been surprised by it. But though the formula was the same its meaning changed, and "truth carried alive into the heart by passion" does not always mean to Wordsworth what it would have meant, in practice, to any number of eighteenth-century advocates of the sublime.

A partial result of such values in eighteenth-century poetry was a literature of energetic picture-making but of little drama because the drama in which the reader was invited to participate was within his own mind, a drama of response, an exaltation that came on the imagistic wings of terror and surprise, wonder and admiration. A poetry evocative of such feelings customarily employed character as a way of registering feelings upon the fine instrument of a receptive sensibility; character became in the works of the mid-century poets an exponent of feeling, showing how it felt to be possessed of such emotions, and through sympathy the reader participated in the ectasies of the rapt imagination.

That advocates of the sublime were not neglectful of the human image we have seen in Joseph Warton's comments on "Alexander's Feast," on "Eloisa to Abelard," and especially on "The Bard." However, as Warton's praise for these three poems suggests, critical approbation was largely occasioned by the poets' orchestration of the passions, the delineation of the subjective element in human experience, feeling. Criticism concentrated on the poetic usability of the extraordinary and neglected the ordinary or more probable image of human life. Representations of this kind were left to writers like Goldsmith and Crabbe, and the treatment of men and manners moved increasingly into the domain of prose fiction. The poetry of passion generally failed to provide a contemporary image of man or to recognize the need for one. What was subsequently required was a lyric of greater realism, a lyric not purged of the sublime, but one in which the sublime was disciplined to a psychology not merely credible but often strikingly ordinary. From the ordinary the extraordinary arose, the former providing the basis for the latter, connected with it not merely sequentially but logically or psychologically as well.

Discussing the poetry of Collins, Woodhouse charts the rise of "one romantic theory of poetry, which is content to divorce romance from reality."[10] The justification for this remark resides in the conception of sublimity informing romance; this being so, romance and reality were dissociated, the distended imagination serving as its own justification. Yet, as we have seen, the dissociation was not furthered in the poetry of Blake and Wordsworth, and the fact that it was not suggests a very tightened relation between the ordinary and the extraordinary, between what was felt by the lyric speaker and the ordinary occasions that gave rise to feeling. The relation insisted not only upon a truthful impression of reality but upon making available the causes that underlay vision itself. Thus in "Tintern Abbey" when Wordsworth sees the landscape "connect[ed] . . . with the quiet of the sky," the visualized unity of earth and sky is part of the larger harmony that the speaker seeks between hermit and wood, man and nature. This is why the almost incantatory repetitions with which the poem begins are both act and observation. They signify what is passing inside on the screen of the mind, determining the way in which description will be organized in the poem. The method suggests a substantial part of Wordsworth's realism and implies as well one aspect of the dramatic within the subjective lyric. The repetitions signify what it is we are invited to witness and therefore guide us through the experience that will end, at the conclusion of the poem's first movement, in the summoning of the hermit's unseen presence from the depths of the houseless woods. In Wordsworth's lyric we are continually being recalled to the dramatic basis of the poet's art, to the recognition that his sometimes naive, or urgent, or merely strolling narrator carries within himself a miniature drama, and that the terms of his seeing are the enactment of what lies within.

Thus, to notice again Wordsworth's use of repetitious diction in "Tintern Abbey," the repeated employment of "again," of "green," the slight variations that reintroduce the same word or its synonym in a different context, define the continuity of the speaker's feelings and meditations even as they change. Our reference is to the structure of feeling itself, feeling that shapes itself in the context of a sustained and lengthened psychological moment, and we are given, as in a detective story, the dictional clues that inform the terms of vision. It is the basis of character we seek, finding in language the symptoms of identity, locating the relation between what is said and what is felt.

Johnson remarked in the Preface to the *Dictionary* that "Language is only the instrument of science, and words are but the signs of ideas." The formula was often evaded by the mid-century romancers in their revival of Spenserian or Miltonic diction, in their trust that an antique diction would prove more richly connotative, more suggestive of the passions. Wordsworth's use of diction has little to do with the language really used by men, an idea in itself as futile, if not reactionary, as any to come from the Wartons. But in the "Essay upon Epitaphs—III," Wordsworth states that "if words be not . . . an incarnation of the thought but only a cloathing for it, then surely will they prove an ill gift." In a footnote to "The Thorn" he adds that words are "not only symbols of the passion, but . . . *things,* active and efficient, which are of themselves part of the passion."[11] His effort is to drive language into feeling, to employ language as simultaneously descriptive of what is seen and revelatory of the "passion" which determines the seeing. His attitude toward language is formulated not to enhance picturesque vivacity but to solve the problem of language's affective power that Burke sought in obscurity and others in imagistic boldness and clarity. Wordsworth faces squarely the recognition that language is not only the expression of the poet's consciousness but the medium into which consciousness is translated, an alternative though never wholly satisfactory form.

The mid-century exploitation of the passions had culminated in a poetic diction not merely archaic but, from

Wordsworth's perspective, unnatural, unrealistic, and deadening. In the Appendix to the Preface he offers examples of "misdiction" from one of Thomas Russel's sonnets. Among other terms to which he objects are "unshelter'd," "passing charity," "thy happier lot," "taunting throng," "oppresser's iron scourge," and "heavenly bright." He notes: "The Reader has only to translate this sonnet into such language as any person of good sense and lively sensibility, one, I mean, who does not talk out of books—would use upon such an occasion in real life, and he will at once perceive in what manner the passages printed in italics are defective."[12]

By the middle years of the eighteenth century nothing sounded more bookish than the language of graveyard melancholy. Joseph Warton's Solitude, walking forth in the "deep dead of night," "beneath the pale Moon's light," in "robe of flowing black array'd, / While cypress-leaves thy brows o'ershade," was an apparition all too common. Realism was the one principal element the Wartons commonly sought to exclude from their verse and the reasons are not far to seek. On the one hand realistic characterization (Wordsworth's "person of good sense") was associated with the lyric of ethical and didactic intention. To Joseph Warton, Pope was "the First of Ethical authors in verse." Of this "species of writing" he commented: "It lies more level to the general capacities of men, than the higher flights of more genuine poetry. We all remember when even a *Churchill* was more in vogue than a *Gray*. He that treats of fashionable follies, and the topics of the day, that describes *present persons and recent events,* finds many readers, whose understandings and whose passions he gratifies" (last italics mine).[13]

While the reference is to the use of topical figures in satirical verse, it is also true that such employments made up part of a realistic verse tradition to which Warton objected. The usual oppositions occur. Pope admired French models: "he studied *Boileau* attentively; formed himself upon *him,* as Milton formed himself upon the Grecian and Italian sons of *Fancy.* He stuck to describing modern *manners;* but those *manners,* because they are *familiar, uniform, artificial,* and *polished,* are, in their very nature, unfit for any lofty effort of the Muse."[14] Wordsworth could surely have agreed with some of this, for the "familiar" and the "uniform" he regarded as fit subjects. He valued "repeated experience and regular feelings" because they are antipathetic to the "artificial" and the "polished."

Behind the mid-century writers there was also the tradition of Cowley, Donne, and the metaphysicals. Hurd had published an edition of Cowley's poems in 1772 and was generally appreciative of the "pensiveness" he found characteristic of this poet. But of Donne's lyrics he made the following observation:

> The more august poetry disclaims, as unsuited to its state and dignity, that inquisitive and anxious diligence, which pries into nature's retirements; and searches through all her secret and hidden haunts, to detect a forbidden commerce, and expose to light some strange unexpected conjunction of ideas. This quaint combination of remote, unallied imagery, constitutes a species of entertainment, which, for its *novelty,* may amuse and divert the mind in other compositions; but is wholly inconsistent with the reserve and solemnity of the *graver* forms.[15]

Responding to the badgering of his reviewers, Joseph Warton silently demoted Donne from the "second class" of poets to the third. The third class Warton defined as composed of "men of wit, of elegant taste, and some fancy in describing familiar life."[16] Donne here found place with Butler, Swift, Rochester, Dorset, and Oldham. He was obviously badly miscast in this company, but the objection comes through clearly. In relation to true poetic *gravity,* to the sublime and pathetic, Donne's limitations, though different, were as ex-

tensive as Pope's. Where Pope appealed merely to "the
general capacities of men," Donne strayed into areas of "forbidden commerce" and was "quaint." If one seemed to Warton too modern, too artificial, to found the lyric of passion
upon, the other seemed to Hurd too cerebral, too strained,
too curious. Thus, while the mid-century critics widened remarkably the usable past, they also narrowed it considerably.

Of the poets of the preceding hundred years, Milton was
by far the most influential figure, but the sublimity they
derived from him was limited by what their derivations
excluded. For example, to come down from "Lycidas,"
through Dryden's "Ode on the Death of Mrs. Killigrew," to
Gray's "Elegy" is to recognize the steady diminution of
Christian humanism and Platonic idealism, elements of Miltonic sublimity of which the mid-century poets and critics
could make little use. They were left in an oddly anomalous
situation: they appreciated the sublime and pathetic in some
of Dryden's and Pope's poetry, but invariably they declined
to celebrate the major achievements of that poetry. They
strongly valued "L'Allegro" and "Il Penseroso" but did not
deal at length with the major epics or *Samson Agonistes*. Thus
the poets and critics of mid-century took less than the characteristic excellence offered by their Restoration and Augustan
predecessors and less than the very best from Milton. From
their conception of the essential qualities of poetry—the
marvelous in the service of passion—they derived their poetic. As Rosemond Tuve aptly remarks: "If Milton's hermit in
his mossy cell had a caption it would be neither 'romantic
Middle Ages' nor 'religious touch,' but *Platonic Ascent*."[17]
The musing hermit of Warton's "The Pleasures of Melancholy" would, however, be best identified as *solitary melancholic*. What was taken from Dryden and from Pope, as well
as from Milton, was much less than they had to give. Rather,
the mid-century romancers emphasized the sublime of pas-

sion, a reductionism so limiting that little first-rate poetry was written under its auspices.

Yet what appeared of special value to the age is evident in two facts. Pindar's odes went through more than a half dozen translations between 1748 and 1791. William Smith's translation of Longinus was reprinted nine times between 1739 and 1777. If to some very considerable extent the poets and critics of mid-century opened the way back to Chaucer and Spenser, they nevertheless brought all literature to the test of the sublime and the pathetic. In this regard they were served handsomely by British aesthetics.

As a leading principle, sentiment, of which the sublime was the grandest possible expression, could be justified as an end in and of itself, the poem understood as an organization of emotions. In 1790 Archibald Alison, the most important of the Scottish literary associationists, developed the position that "by means of the Connexion, or Resemblance, which subsists between the qualities of Matter, and qualities capable of producing Emotion, the perception of one immediately and very often irresistibly suggests the idea of the other." There is thus no single perfect form, "or species of Forms, which is fitted by the constitution of our nature immediately to excite the Emotion of Beauty, and independent of all association."[18] Beauty is to be established upon subjective principles, upon associations formed between "certain sensations and certain qualities."[19] Though such associations are subjective they are not merely personal. Rather, they are founded upon what may be called a community of cultural associations. Like others around us we respond to the same symbols, to those qualities to which we have previously observed certain forms attach themselves. For example, listening to a piece of music we do not merely respond to sounds but to those emotional qualities for which the sounds are symbols. The work of art is thus understood as an organization of symbols, each presumably calibrated to affect the listener differently. The artist *plays* on his listener's emotions by arranging the relations among the symbols into patterns to produce the effect he seeks. These patterns constitute the structure of the composition; structure is an affective organization.

Not only do material qualities possess no beauty in and of themselves, but as symbols they derive their beauty from the expressions of mind: "The qualities of matter become significant to us of those qualities of mind which are destined to affect us with pleasing or interesting emotion."[20] The principle of sympathy had been linked with the imagination by Adam Smith, and Alexander Gerard had defined the imagination as a "medium, through which the passions or dominant associations operate in an almost magnetic creation or response."[21] Alison, returning to this conception, which was very common among the faculty psychologists in the 1760s and 1770s, employed the principle of sympathy to explain the direct and immediate way in which the symbol affects us and awakens the mind to trains of fascinating imagery. The material qualities are "the signs of all those Affections . . . which we love, or with which we are formed to sympathize." Such affections are the "*direct* expressions of Mind; and the material qualities which signify [them] . . . produce in us immediately the peculiar emotions which, by the laws of our nature, the mental qualities are fitted to produce."[22]

However interesting Alison's psychology, it pointed backward and not forward, toward those aesthetic categories of which the eighteenth-century theorists were so fond: the sublime, the picturesque, and the beautiful. The grading and classifying of phenomena were carried on tirelessly through the middle and later years of the century and sometimes resembled a geometry of aesthetics. Henry Home, for example, had observed that "a square . . . is less beautiful than a circle," because in the former "the attention is divided among the sides and angles . . . whereas the circumference of a circle, being a single object, makes one entire impression."[23]

Georges Poulet seizes upon the image of the circle, using Addison's example of an architectural concavity for the generalizations that he, Poulet, wishes to draw from it:

Addison speaks no differently than Plotinus, Saint Augustine, Saint Bonaventura, or Marsile Ficin. Yet for these last named, the final reason for this beauty was the analogy between the center of the circle and the divine unity whose infinite richness radiated in creation. Therein lay an eminently theological reason. For the writer of the eighteenth century there could be no question of reasoning in this way. The circle is beautiful because, from the center where he situates it, man's eye can easily embrace the whole shape of it. Such is the explication given by Addison. It comes from a thought which cannot place itself except in the domain of psychological relativism and of perspectivism.[24]

Addison's thought is consistent with the ontology offered by some aesthetic forms and by some natural forms, both of which were recognized as sublime. For Addison the sublime is what remains of the occasion for transcendence in an age in which religion is demythologized. The sublime object evokes the proper psychological response—enthusiasm. The literary associationists of the age, among whom Addison must certainly be numbered, explored and, as time went on, often merely reiterated the psychological bases for such response. The circle is both a metaphor for Creation and a metaphor for scientific or rational order. God as geometer. Blake recognized the eighteenth-century observance of such truths in his illustration of the compass-wielding Urizen. A demythologized literature, of the kind against which Blake was reacting, may well tend to celebrate mathematics as divine order and validate the power and grandeur of that order through the evocation of wonder and astonishment.

The distended imagination leads to two premises of feeling consequent upon the sublime. One is to be identified with

Collins, Gray, and the Wartons. Within this tradition, feeling
is delineated in its many varieties and represented through
such modes as personification and *ut pictura poesis*. It is the
tradition of the secular sublime. The other, inclusive of Akenside, Young, Smart, and Cowper, is that of the religious sublime, the poetry of Christian supernaturalism wherein feeling
is made the agent of religious conviction and Shaftesburian
rapture enlisted as the vehicle of belief. Both traditions
coexist in eighteenth-century poetry, though the latter has
until recently received scant attention from modern scholars.[25] Fussell's comment is typical: "The whole contemporary attempt to pump some life into a new Christian poetry,
from the theorizing of John Dennis to the practice of Smart
and the hymnodists, betrays its impossibility by its self-
consciousness. The more Dennis argues and speculates, the
more hymns Wesley and Cowper grind out, the more clearly
they reveal that the atmosphere in which they find themselves is not favourable to either traditional Christianity or
traditional elegy."[26] Agreed, but the diminished vitality of
Christian poetry within the century has nevertheless a life of
sorts, and through this half-life the poetry of Christian
supernaturalism was at least maintained within the age. The
truth seems to be that the poetry of secular and religious
sublimity coexisted but did not coalesce, and it remained for
Blake and Wordsworth to perform this urgent task through
the recreation of the dramatic and subjective lyric.

  In reconstructing the Miltonic theme of innocence and
experience, Blake and Wordsworth recreate a lyric poetry
focused primarily upon those mental events that find their
locus in either state of the soul. In doing so both poets translate, it seems fair to say, the epic theme of *Paradise Lost* into its
lyric form and rewrite for their own age the Adamic experience through the new everyman of their lyric protagonists.
Wordsworth's early lyrics, unlike Blake's, are more specifically elegiac, yet in so far as the *Songs of Experience* stands as

an end to innocence it too signifies recognitions decidedly elegiac. More importantly, however, both poets write a literature newly phylogenic, recording the natural or symbolic history of man's growth from innocence to experience and expressive of those common facts of feeling that mark man's progress from one state to another.[27] Wordsworth's poetry is more overtly elegiac because what for Blake is a symbolic fact is for Wordsworth more clearly a natural one. Thus, Wordsworth's man is preeminently rustic, or poet-in-the-world, man coming to the self-understanding that the natural facts of experience, loss, decline, and death, impose upon him. The difference between the poets is therefore more minor than it may seem initially.

Along with Blake, Wordsworth finds his principal subject in the trial of becoming fully human, which is what the passage from innocence to experience signifies. Unlike the poets of mid-century, both Blake and Wordsworth find a subject within subjectivism and thereby create the human image in response to the reexperienced Fall. For both, the Fall is into common nature, registered on our sensibilities, and definitive of our common humanity, the problem of our nature. The Fall is not merely a catastrophe of prehistory but a continuing occurrence and therefore a natural and dramatic event. Wordsworth does not finally arrange his poetry in such a way as to make this subject clear to us, and the 1815 edition of his poems obscures the progress of his thought from the *Lyrical Ballads* of 1798 to the *Poems in Two Volumes* of 1807.[28] Yet the progress is there, and the great elegiac "Ode" of the 1807 edition fittingly concludes the volumes as it terminates the progress.

With this collection of Wordsworth's poems chiefly in mind, Hazlitt decided:

The great fault of a modern school of poetry is, that it is an experiment to reduce poetry to a mere effusion of natural sensibility; or what is worse, to divest it both of imaginary splendour and human passion, to surround the meanest objects with the morbid feelings and devouring egotism of the writers' own minds. Milton and Shakespeare did not so understand poetry. They gave a more liberal interpretation both to nature and art. They did not do all they could to get rid of the one and the other, to fill up the dreary void with the Moods of their own Minds.[29]

The statement suggests perhaps the largest possible misunderstanding of the Wordsworthian lyric and the necessities that shaped it. Those "Moods" to which Hazlitt referred so scornfully are recollective of innocence, and it is no accident of ordering that the section titled "Moods of My Own Mind" ends with a meditation on transcendence:

> It is no Spirit who from Heaven hath flown,
> And is descending on his embassy;
> Nor Traveller gone from Earth the Heavens to espy!
> 'Tis Hesperus—there he stands with glittering crown,
> First admonition that the sun is down!
> For yet it is broad day-light: clouds pass by;
> A few are near him still—and now the sky,
> He hath it to himself—'tis all his own.
> O most ambitious Star! an inquest wrought
> Within me when I recognized thy light;
> A moment was I startled at the sight:
> And, while I gazed, there came to me a thought
> That I might step beyond my natural race
> As thou seem'st now to do; might one day trace
> Some ground not mine; and, strong her strength above,
> My Soul, an Apparition in the place,
> Tread there, with steps that no one shall reprove!

Like Hesperus, the imagination is an admonitory light, illuminative in M. H. Abrams's sense, "ambitious" to irradiate the common human condition.

Barbara Lewalski remarks tellingly that the theme of innocence in *Paradise Lost* "is an exaltation of humanism, maturity, civilization in happiest conjunction with vitality, change, growth. Such an imagination of the State of Innocence sets the Fall in the proper tragic perspective in the poem, as the event which blasted man's opportunity to develop—without suffering, violence, despair and death, though not in the least without tension and trial—the rich resources and large potentialities of the human spirit."[30] Returning to this theme, Blake and Wordsworth alter it strikingly. Suffering, violence, despair, and death are precisely what must be endured in experience; the resources of the human spirit are the focus of any number of Blake's and Wordsworth's characterizations: of Lyca, of Thel, of Oothoon; of the Leech-gatherer, the mature speaker of "There was a Boy," the revisiter of "Tintern Abbey," and the poet of the "Ode." Such characters are, in a sense shared by both Blake and Wordsworth, permanent images of man, permanent because through them the resources of the human spirit in experience are tested in ways that are eternal and inevitable. The earthly unparadise of experience requires that feeling be translated into knowledge, and the journey from one state to another tests by challenging the capacities of the human sensibility.

As a marvelous journey it is not a fiction, for probability is the soul of it; it is what the experiencing intelligence must come to. As such the theme corresponds to, or inaugurates, all the various journeys of Romantic poetry, of *The Ancient Mariner,* of *Endymion,* of *Alastor.* Its common action is the soul in search of itself, feeling the stages of its progress and registering its gains as the accumulated triumphs of self-consciousness. Through this theme a Milton greater than that known by the mid-century poets is given again to English poetry and one Miltonic revival succeeds another.[31] A just and lively image of human nature is renewed in an image both probable and marvelous.

Upon an assumed community of feeling, Wordsworth confidently builds his lyric, sure of the recognition that ultimately awaits him, certain of the universal truths that underlie and give meaning to his work. Like Blake he seeks the marvelous within human nature, sanctified by the poet as prophet, speaking not like Gray's bard of distant dooms but of the garden and grave that lie within. A century earlier Dennis had said that "Poetry is the natural Language of Religion," adding as a cautionary observation that "the less mixture that Religion has of any thing profane and human in it, the greater Warmth and Passion it must give to Poetry."[32] The truth seen equally by Blake and Wordsworth is that the human is extraordinary witness to the divine, and the road of experience leads to the palace of wisdom.

Notes

1 · Introduction

1. Northrop Frye, "Towards Defining an Age of Sensibility," *ELH* 23 (1956): 144–52.
2. Stuart Chase, *Quest for Myth*, p. 21; Louis Bredvold, *The Natural History of Sensibility*, p. 101; Bertrand Bronson, "When Was Neoclassicism?" in *Studies in Criticism and Aesthetics, 1660–1800*, p. 35.
3. Samuel Monk, *The Sublime*, p. 238.
4. Ian Watt, "The Comic Syntax of *Tristam Shandy*," in *Studies in Criticism and Aesthetics, 1660–1800*, pp. 328–29; J. B. Beer, *Coleridge the Visionary*, p. 267.

2 · The Critical Situation

1. Thomas Hobbes, "Answer to Davenant," in *Critical Essays of the Seventeenth Century*, ed. J. E. Spingarn, 2:59; Hobbes, *Leviathan*, p. 43; Thomas Shadwell, Preface to *The Humorists*, Spingarn, 2:159; Richard Blackmore, Preface to *Prince Arthur*, Spingarn, 3:238.
2. Hobbes, "Answer to Davenant," Spingarn, 2:62; Robert Wolseley, Preface to *Valentinian*, Spingarn, 3:21, 22; William Davenant, Preface to *Gondibert*, Spingarn, 2:5; Hobbes, "Answer to Davenant," p. 61; William Temple, "Of Poetry," Spingarn, 3:96.
3. Abraham Cowley, Preface to *Poems*, Spingarn, 2:88; Davenant, Preface to *Gondibert*, Spingarn, 2:11; Edward Phillips, Preface to *Theatrum Poetarum*, Spingarn, 2:268.
4. Preface to "Rapin," *The Critical Works of Thomas Rymer*, p. 5.
5. Rymer, "A Short View of Tragedy," *Critical Works*, p. 134; John Dryden, "Defence of the Epilogue," *Essays*, 1:165; Joseph Addison, *The Spectator*, 3:145; Samuel Johnson, "Life of Milton," *Lives of the English Poets*, 1:163.

6. Thomas Warton, *Observations on the Fairy Queen,* 1:15; Richard Hurd, "A Dissertation on the Idea of Universal Poetry," *Eighteenth-Century Critical Essays,* ed. Scott Elledge, 2: 863, 862; Hurd, *Letters on Chivalry and Romance,* pp. 93–94; Joseph Warton, *An Essay on the Genius and Writings of Pope,* 1:26, 2:16, 1:vi; Hugh Blair, "A Critical Dissertation on the Poems of Ossian," *The Poems of Ossian,* 2:323; Robert Lowth, *Lectures on the Sacred Poetry of the Hebrews,* 2:68.

7. T. Warton, *Observations,* 2:53; Hurd, *Letters,* pp. 55, 120, 60; J. Warton, *Essay on Pope,* 2:29, 343–44, 167.

8. T. Warton, *Observations,* 2:101–2; T. Warton, *The History of English Poetry,* 1:xxiv, lxxi, 2:175.

9. Hurd, *Letters,* p. 31; J. Warton, *Essay on Pope,* 2:3–4; Warton, *Observations,* 1:188, 197.

10. T. Warton, *History,* 4:332.

11. Ernest Tuveson, *The Imagination as a Means of Grace,* pp. 76–77.

12. Clarence Thorpe, *The Aesthetic Theory of Thomas Hobbes,* p. 289.

13. Francis Bacon, "Advancement of Learning," *Works,* 1:88; Hobbes, *Leviathan,* p. 43.

14. *Spectator,* 3:560.

15. Ibid., p. 561.

16. Ibid., p. 563.

17. Ibid., p. 571.

18. Tuveson, *The Imagination as a Means of Grace,* pp. 80–84.

19. *Spectator,* 3:573.

20. Ibid., p. 578.

21. Hurd, *Letters,* pp. 91–92; Warton, *Essay on Pope,* 1:265; Blair, *Poems of Ossian,* 2:284.

22. John Husbands, Preface to *A Miscellany of Poems by Several Hands,* p. 16; Thomas Blackwell, *An Inquiry into the Life and Writings of Homer,* p. 26; Joseph Trapp, *Lectures on Poetry,* p. 338.

23. Trapp, *Lectures,* p. 351.

24. Preface to *A Miscellany,* p. 31.

25. Pope, Preface to *Iliad,* Elledge, 1:267, 538; Trapp, *Lectures,* p. 338; Pope, Preface to the *Works of Shakespeare, Literary Criticism of Alexander Pope,* p. 163.

26. *The Critical Works of Thomas Rymer,* ed. Curt Zimansky, p. xxiv.

27. Temple, "Of Poetry," Spingarn, 3:96.

28. Hurd, "A Dissertation on Universal Poetry," Elledge, 1:863; J. Warton, *Essay on Pope*, 1:355, vi; T. Warton, *History*, 3:285; Hurd, *Letters*, pp. 80, 81.

29. Earl Miner, "Mr. Dryden and Mr. Rymer," *PQ* 54 (1975): 144–45.

30. "The Grounds of Criticism in Poetry," *The Critical Works of John Dennis*, 1:363, 364.

31. T. Warton, *Observations*, 1:196.

32. T. Warton, *History*, 1:lxxiii.

33. Ibid., 3:284–85, 286, 4:328.

34. Hurd, "A Dissertation on Universal Poetry," Elledge, 2:863; Blair, *Poems of Ossian*, 2:324.

35. T. Warton, ed., *Poems upon Several Occasions . . . by John Milton*, p. iv; Robert Lowth, *Lectures on the Sacred Poetry of the Hebrews*, 1:20; J. Warton, ed., *The Poetical Works of John Dryden*, p. 168n; Edward Young, "On Lyric Poetry," Elledge, 1:413.

3 · Mid-Century Poets

1. *The Percy Letters*, p. 48.

2. *Correspondence of Thomas Gray*, 1:261.

3. T. Warton, *Observations*, 2:91–92.

4. Johnson, Preface to Shakespeare, *Works*, 7:96–98.

5. "Life of Collins," *Lives*, 3:337.

6. Jean Hagstrum, *The Sister Arts*, p. 272.

7. P. M. Spacks suggests that "Collins lacked the theory to justify his practice fully, but his practice belongs to a grand poetic tradition" (*The Poetry of Vision*, p. 82). Despite her very able explication of Collins's poetry, Professor Spacks is, I believe, mistaken in the first part of her observation.

8. Roger Lonsdale, ed., *The Poems of Gray, Collins, and Goldsmith*, pp. 414–15.

9. J. R. Crider, "Structure and Effect in Collins's Progress Poems" *SP* 60 (1963): 60.

10. Ricardo Quintana, "The Scheme of Collins's *Odes on Several . . . Subjects*," *Restoration and Eighteenth-Century Literature*, ed. Carroll Camden, p. 376.

11. J. Warton, *Adventurer*, no. 57, *The British Essayists*, 24:92.

12. Arthur Johnston, *Enchanted Ground*, pp. 9–10.

13. T. Warton, *Observations,* 2:268; Johnson, *Works,* 7:64, 4:285.

14. Blair, "A Critical Dissertation on the Poems of Ossian," 2:375, 416.

15. *The Miniature,* no. 2, 30 April 1804; cited by Johnston, p. 201.

16. Johnson, *Works,* 4:286.

17. A.S.P. Woodhouse, "The Poetry of Collins Reconsidered," *From Sensibility to Romanticism,* F. W. Hilles and Harold Bloom, eds., p. 126.

18. Chester Chapin has very accurately observed that the "odes of Collins, taken as a whole, represent the most thoroughgoing attempt in eighteenth-century poetry at the evocation of images 'without any foundation in reality.' This was the result of Collins's wholehearted acceptance of the Wartonian pronouncement that 'invention and imagination' are the 'chief faculties of a poet'" (*Personification in Eighteenth-Century English Poetry,* p. 45). See Chapin's entire discussion of this subject under the heading "The Personified Abstraction as a 'Fiction of the Mind'" (pp. 31–51).

19. In *The Insistence of Horror* P. M. Spacks remarks that "if the mind of man is naturally subject to secret terrors and apprehensions, if such beings as ghosts and witches are inevitable symbols of these fears, it is clearly difficult to pretend that the ghostly is interesting as a subject only at a distance, that it has to do only with the unsophisticated intelligence; for in fact it has profound significance—even if only symbolically—for *all* men. The history of the uses of the supernatural in eighteenth-century poetry seems, when one looks back over it, to be a history of struggles with this realization; and when the realization was fully achieved, the Romantic Age was at hand" (p. 196). It is possible, and desirable, to agree with much of this, yet it is difficult, at the same time, to know what recognitions the conclusion asserts or masks.

20. Jean Hagstrum, *Samuel Johnson's Literary Criticism,* pp. 99, 101. Hagstrum relates these terms to "Johnson's acceptance of the familiar theory of neoclassical literary history that the line of greatest technical development in English verse began with Waller and Denham and culminated in Dryden and Pope. . . . Johnson's is therefore what Mr. Bateson calls a 'negative' and not a 'positive' theory of poetic diction, less important for what it recommends than for what it forbids. In Mr. Bateson's words, the Augustan

poets 'tended therefore to avoid familiar words because of the un-manageable range of their associations and unfamiliar words for the opposite reason that they had next to no associations at all.'" Hagstrum adds: "Such a theory separated Johnson from those who attempted to achieve dictional beauty by widening the difference between prose and poetry—the imitators of Milton, Spenser, and the Greeks."

21. Johnson, *Lives*, 3:338, 341, 434, 440.

22. Paul Fussell, *The Rhetorical World of Augustan Humanism*, pp. 6, 20.

23. Hagstrum, *Samuel Johnson's Literary Criticism*, p. 143; Johnson, *The History of Rasselas, Prince of Abissinia*, chap. 44; Johnson, *The Rambler*, no. 137, *Works*, 4:360; Duff, *An Essay on Original Genius*, p. 270.

24. *The Prose Works of William Wordsworth*, 3: 83, 82.

25. Norman Maclean, "From Action to Image: Theories of the Lyric in the Eighteenth Century," *Critics and Criticism*, ed. R. S. Crane, p. 440; M. H. Abrams, *The Mirror and the Lamp*, p. 290.

26. *Lives*, 3:441–42.

27. Frye, "Towards Defining an Age of Sensibility," pp. 144–52.

28. Cf. W. J. Bate, *The Burden of the Past and the English Poet*.

29. F. Doherty, "The Two Voices of Gray," *EC* 13 (1963): 222–30.

30. Coleridge, *Biographia Literaria*, 1:13; Spacks, "Artful Strife: Conflict in Gray's Poetry," *PMLA* 81 (1966): 69; Doherty, "The Two Voices of Gray," p. 225; Arnold, *Essays in Criticism*, pp. 92–93.

31. *Correspondence of Thomas Gray*, 2:541, 571, 3:1018.

32. Roger Lonsdale, ed., *The Poems of Gray, Collins, and Goldsmith*, pp. 48–53.

33. William Shenstone, *The Works in Verse and Prose*, 1:6.

34. There are a number of excellent works dealing with the subject of personification in eighteenth-century English poetry. Along with P. M. Spacks's *The Insistence of Horror* and Chester Chapin's *Personification in Eighteenth-Century English Poetry* there are most usefully Bertrand Bronson's "Personification Reconsidered" (available in his *Facets of the Enlightenment*), and Earl Wasserman's response, "The Inherent Values of Eighteenth-Century Personification," *PMLA* 65 (1950): 435–63. Bronson's essay is a very subtle exposition and appreciation of different kinds of personifica-

tion. It is perhaps unfortunate therefore that he allows oppositions between eighteenth-century subtlety and "Romantic egoism" (p. 150) to invade his discussion.

35. David Hartley, *Observations on Man*, 1:427.
36. *Lives*, 3:438; *The Correspondence and Other Papers of James Boswell Relating to the Making of the Life of Johnson*, pp. 311, 312.
37. J. Warton, *Essay on Pope*, 2:405; Addison, *Spectator*, 3:144.
38. *The Poems of Gray, Collins, and Goldsmith*, pp. 180–81.
39. J. Warton, *Essay on Pope*, 1:295, 301.
40. Ibid., pp. 375–76n.
41. Ibid.
42. Ibid., p. 330.
43. Nathan Drake, *Literary Hours* (London, 1798), pp. 250, 379; cited by Monk, *The Sublime*, p. 137.
44. J. Warton, ed., *The Poetical Works of John Dryden*, p. 168n.
45. *Correspondence of Thomas Gray*, 2: 664, 679–80, 693.
46. Ibid., 3:1290.
47. The most adequate study of the importance of the Wartons is Joan Pittock's *The Ascendancy of Taste*.
48. Maclean, "From Action to Image," p. 445.
49. Abraham Tucker, *The Light of Nature Pursued*, 1:14. The first three volumes of *The Light of Nature Pursued* were published in 1768; three more followed in 1778. This citation is from the two-volume 1852 edition.
50. Archibald Alison, *Essays on the Nature and Principles of Taste*, 1:58–59.
51. Charles Avison, *Essays on Poetry and Music*, p. 3; Brown, cited in Abrams, *The Mirror and the Lamp*, p. 93; Edmund Burke, *A Philosophical Enquiry into the Origins of our Ideas of the Sublime and Beautiful*, p. 60; William Jones, "On the Arts Commonly Called Imitative," Elledge, 2:881.

4 · William Blake

1. Northrop Frye, *Fearful Symmetry*, pp. 167, 171.
2. Irene Tayler, *Blake's Illustrations to the Poems of Gray*, p. 34.
3. Tayler, p. 39; John Grant, "Envisioning the First *Night Thoughts*," *Blake's Visionary Forms Dramatic*, eds. David Erdman and John Grant, pp. 332–33.
4. Kathleen Raine, *Blake and Tradition*, 1:125.

5. "Life of Milton," *Lives*, 1:174. Johnson's general objections to religious poetry are well known. He commonly regards religion as a subject for which poetry is unfit: "Such events as were produced by the visible interposition of Divine Power are above the power of human genius to dignify" ("Life of Cowley," 1:50). He makes a similar observation in regard to *Paradise Lost:* "The good and evil of Eternity are too ponderous for the wings of wit; the mind sinks under them in passive helplessness, content with calm belief and humble adoration" ("Life of Milton," 1:182).

6. David B. Morris, *The Religious Sublime*, p. 171.

7. It is becoming increasingly apparent, as scholars familiarize themselves with Blake's designs for eighteenth-century poetry, that his illustrations more often than not suggest a revision of the obvious textual intentions. Cf., T. H. Helmstadter, "Blake's *Night Thoughts*," *TSLL* 12 (1970): 27–54.

8. *Correspondence of Thomas Gray*, 1:423–24, 2:802, 1:224.

9. Abbie Findlay Potts, *Wordsworth's "Prelude."* Such topics as "Pope's *Essay on Criticism* and Wordsworth's Critical Essays," "*Dunciad* IV and *Prelude* III and V," "Beattie's Edwin and Young William Wordsworth," "William Rereads *The Castle of Indolence*," and "The *Recluse-Prelude-Excursion* and *Night Thoughts*," signify Professor Potts's conception of Wordsworth's indebtedness to his predecessors; Raine, *Blake and Tradition*.

10. S. F. Bolt, "The Songs of Innocence," *William Blake: Songs of Innocence and Experience*, ed. Margaret Bottrall, p. 114.

11. E. D. Hirsch, *Innocence and Experience*, p. 114; Robert Gleckner, "Point of View and Context in Blake's Songs," Bottrall, pp. 195–96.

12. David Erdman, ed., *The Prose and Poetry of William Blake*, p. 714; Hirsch, *Innocence and Experience*, pp. 30, 36, 186, 26.

13. Martin Nurmi, "Fact and Symbol in 'The Chimney Sweeper' of Blake's *Songs of Innocence*," *BNYPL* 68 (1964); reprinted in *Blake: A Collection of Critical Essays*, ed. Northrop Frye, p. 21; Gleckner, "Point of View and Context in Blake's Songs," Bottrall, p. 196.

14. Harold Bloom, *Blake's Apocalypse*, pp. 37, 41.

15. Ibid., p. 48.

16. Ibid.

17. Robert Gleckner, *The Piper and the Bard*, p. 99.

18. Jean Hagstrum, *William Blake*, p. 83.

19. There is an extensive literature on the subject of Christian belief and English Romanticism, much of it in relation to Wordsworth. The introduction to Richard Brantley's *Wordsworth's "Natural Methodism"* competently surveys, in text and notes, the character of past and present scholarly opinion on this subject. The darker aspect of Romanticism, the "erotic sensibility," has been more than adequately surveyed by Mario Praz in *The Romantic Agony*. Despite Praz's thesis, I do not view his topic as independent of that heterodox Christianity of which I have spoken in the text, or, for that matter, of those passions that find expression in the mid-century romancers. Eroticism is a fascinating component of Experience, of that opposition to love and unity, and must somehow be reconciled with them.

20. Frye, *Fearful Symmetry*, p. 177; Raine, *Blake and Tradition*, 1:3.

21. T. S. Eliot, *Selected Essays*, pp. 279, 280.

22. Burke, *A Philosophical Enquiry*, p. 62.

23. Duff, *An Essay on Original Genius*, pp. 6–7.

24. Hobbes, "Answer to Davenant," Spingarn, 2:59.

25. *The Poetry and Prose of William Blake*, p. 573.

26. Ibid., pp. 3–4.

27. Ibid., pp. 586, 593, 592.

28. See Hazard Adams, *William Blake*, pp. 13–15, for a discussion of Blake's realism.

5 · William Wordsworth

1. Francis Jeffrey, *Edinburgh Review*, April 1808; reprinted in *Contemporary Reviews of Romantic Poetry*, ed. John Wain, p. 58.

2. Ralph Cohen, *The Art of Discrimination*, p. 197; William Cowper, *Correspondence*, ed. Thomas Wright (London, 1904), 2:252–53; cited by P. M. Spacks, *The Poetry of Vision*, p. 177.

3. Oliver Sigworth, *William Collins*, p. 72.

4. Elizabeth Manwaring, *Italian Landscape in Eighteenth-Century England*, p. 186.

5. Thomas West, *A Guide to the Lakes*, 1778; cited by Manwaring, p. 194.

6. Alison, *Essays on the Nature and Principles of Taste*, 1:187, 2:417.

7. "On Poetry in General," *The Complete Works of William Hazlitt*, 5:3.

8. The phrase is Kenneth Burke's; for the paces through which he puts it consult *The Philosophy of Literary Form*, pp. 89–102.

9. Josephine Miles, *Eras and Modes in English Poetry*, p. 123.

10. Frye, "Towards Defining an Age of Sensibility," p. 151; Blair, *Lectures on Rhetoric and Belles Lettres*, 2:376; Woodhouse, "The Poetry of Collins Reconsidered," Hilles and Bloom, pp. 112–13.

11. Quintana, "The Scheme of Collins's *Odes on Several . . . Subjects*," Camden, p. 377.

12. Frye, "Towards Defining an Age of Sensibility," p. 151.

13. John Gilbert Cooper, *Letters Concerning Taste*, p. 3.

14. Daniel Webb, *Remarks on the Beauties of Poetry*, p. 86.

15. Duff, *An Essay on Original Genius*, p. 7.

16. Monk, *The Sublime*, p. 85; Burke, *A Philosophical Enquiry*, J. T. Boulton, ed., p. lxxv; Ernst Cassirer, *The Philosophy of the Enlightenment*, p. 330.

17. Geoffrey Hartman, *Wordsworth's Poetry, 1787–1814*, p. 147.

18. *Le Beau Monde*, vol. 2, October 1807; cited by John Hayden, *The Romantic Reviewers, 1802–1824*, p. 82.

19. W. J. Bate, *From Classic to Romantic*, p. 156.

20. July 1807; cited by Hayden, p. 82.

21. Jeffrey, *Edinburgh Review*, vol. 24, November 1814; cited by Hayden, p. 88.

22. William Empson, *Seven Types of Ambiguity*, p. vi.

23. Alexander Knox, *The Flapper*, no. 38, 11 June 1796, Elledge, 2:1115.

24. Ian Jack, *Augustan Satire*, pp. 35–36.

25. Frye, "Towards Defining an Age of Sensibility," p. 150.

26. Jeffrey, *Edinburgh Review*, April 1808; cited in *Contemporary Reviews of Romantic Poetry*, ed. John Wain, p. 57.

27. I am aware of the truth of Bronson's remark that "personification allowed them [i.e., eighteenth-century poets] to recapture the most valuable part of the immediacy of personal statement. It allowed them to make the best of both worlds, the public and the private, to be at the same time general and specific, abstract and concrete" ("Personification Reconsidered," *Facets of the Enlightenment*, p. 147). My comments, however, are intended to suggest the view from Romanticism.

28. *The Prose Works of William Wordsworth*, 1:116, 3: 31, 32, 33, 36, 37; *The Poetical Works of William Wordsworth*, 2:512.

29. *Prose Works*, 3:37–38.

30. W. J. B. Owen, *Wordsworth as Critic*, p. 176.

31. Preface to *Lyrical Ballads*, *Prose Works*, 1:138.

32. *Poetical Works*, 2:331.

33. Preface to *Lyrical Ballads*, *Prose Works*, 1:124, 124n; Appendix, 1:164.

34. Preface to *Lyrical Ballads*, *Prose Works*, 1:143, 142.

35. David Ferry remarks that "Wordsworth's yearning for an uncorrupted experience of the eternal is so intense and powerful that it ends in the devaluation of our ordinary experience, even in the desire for its destruction. . . . Wordsworth is not a great lover of man but almost a great despiser of him" (*The Limits of Mortality*, p. 52). This is a passage to be taken with considerable caution, especially in view of the fact that the speaker in Wordsworth's poems is commonly an actor in the drama and engaged in the arduous task of coming to terms with his own imperfect humanity. It seems unwise to suggest that Wordsworth does not present this activity sympathetically. The Lucy poems alone establish the point.

36. Mark Reed, *Wordsworth*, pp. 347–48.

37. *Prose Works*, 1:139.

38. "Annotations to Wordsworth's Poems," *The Poetry and Prose of William Blake*, p. 654.

39. Blake, "Annotations to Wordsworth's 'Preface' to *The Excursion*," *Poetry and Prose*, p. 656; Hartman, *Wordsworth's Poetry, 1787–1814*, pp. 267, 350.

40. Since writing these and the immediately following lines, I have come upon Jared Curtis's equally brief comments on the resemblance of "The Mental Traveller" to Wordsworth's "Ode" (*Wordsworth's Experiments with Tradition*, p. 126). I have let my observation remain, however, for the purpose it serves in the discussion.

41. *Prose Works*, 1:139.

42. There are a number of works dealing with religious patterns of thought in Wordsworth's poetry. They are summarized briefly in *The English Romantic Poets*, ed. Frank Jordan, pp. 105–8. M. H. Abrams's statement is perhaps closest to prevailing opinion. He speaks of "the assimiliation and reinterpretation of religious ideas, as constitutive elements in a world view founded on secular premises," and the "displacement from a supernatural to a natural frame of reference" (*Natural Supernaturalism*, p. 13).

43. *The Letters of William and Dorothy Wordsworth*, 2:618.

44. Richard Brantley argues the case for "Wordsworth and Evangelical Anglicanism" in *Wordsworth's "Natural Methodism,"* pp. 1–12. My own views are closer to those of Stephen Prickett. His sensitive reading of lines 50–105 in book thirteen of Wordsworth's *Prelude* (1805) leads him to remark that the "failure to understand what Wordsworth and Coleridge meant by 'Imagination' has resulted in a process of progressive 'mystification' by which such phrases as 'the invisible world' are made to bear a variety of mystical interpretations—pantheist, Platonic, and Christian." Prickett, citing line 105 ("To hold communion with the invisible world"), states that "Wordsworth is not using 'communion' loosely to mean 'communication' but in its theological sense of a sacrament. The inanimate world is apprehended directly as a personal encounter." See *Coleridge and Wordsworth,* pp. 37–42.

6 · Conclusion

1. Monk, *The Sublime,* p. 233.

2. Recently the sublime has been attracting renewed attention from scholars approaching the subject largely from the perspective of Romanticism. Albert Wlecke's *Wordsworth and the Sublime* offers in two central chapters what he calls "notes toward . . . a phenomenology of the sublime" (p. 10). An ambitious study by the late Thomas Weiskel, *The Romantic Sublime,* inquires into what may be termed the psychoanalytical history of the sublime in the later eighteenth and early nineteenth centuries. Both studies, in their concern with the "psychology of transcendence" (I quote from Weiskel's half-title), are very different from the more traditional historical inquiries by S. H. Monk, M. H. Nicolson, and W. J. Hipple. Among recent studies see also Stuart A. Ende, *Keats and the Sublime.*

3. Angus Fletcher, *Allegory,* p. 247; John Gilbert Cooper, *Letters Concerning Taste,* letter 7; Abrams, *The Mirror and the Lamp,* p. 133.

4. Friedrich Schiller, "The Sublime," *Essays Aesthetical and Philosophical* (London, 1882), p. 133; cited by Fletcher, p. 267.

5. Alexander Gerard, *An Essay on Genius,* p. 68.

6. Thomas Twining, "On Poetry Considered as an Imitative Art," Elledge, 2:990.

7. Fussell, *The Rhetorical World of Augustan Humanism,* p. 15; Addison, *Spectator,* 2:587.

8. Duff, *An Essay on Original Genius*, pp. 150, 152; Daniel Webb, *An Inquiry into the Beauties of Painting*, p. 45; Frances Reynolds, *An Inquiry Concerning the Principles of Taste, and the Origin of our Ideas of Beauty*, pp. 18, 19.

9. Burke, *A Philosophical Enquiry*, p. 60; Jones, "On the Arts Commonly Called Imitative," Elledge, 2:881.

10. Woodhouse, "The Poetry of Collins Reconsidered," Hilles and Bloom, p. 104.

11. *Prose Works*, 2:84; *Poetical Works*, 2:513.

12. *Prose Works*, 1:163.

13. J. Warton, *Essay on Pope*, 2:403.

14. Ibid., 402.

15. Richard Hurd, *Q. Horatii Flacci Epistolae ad Pisones et Augustum*, 3:97–98.

16. *Essay on Pope*, 1:vii.

17. Tuve, *Images and Themes in Five Poems by Milton*, p. 32.

18. Alison, *Essays on the Nature and Principles of Taste*, 1:187, 358.

19. Tuveson, *The Imagination as a Means of Grace*, p. 188. See pp. 186–98 for Tuveson's discussion of Alison and the new language of symbolism. My view of Alison's importance differs substantially from Professor Tuveson's.

20. Alison, *Essays on the Nature and Principles of Taste*, 2:417.

21. W. J. Bate, *From Classic to Romantic*, p. 141.

22. Alison, *Essays on the Nature and Principles of Taste*, 2:419.

23. Henry Home, *Elements of Criticism*, p. 105.

24. Georges Poulet, *The Metamorphoses of the Circle*, p. 59.

25. A very useful recent study is David Morris's *The Religious Sublime*.

26. Fussell, *The Rhetorical World of Augustan Humanism*, p. 285.

27. Though it has not been my intention to give Coleridge's poetry a significant place in this study it is worth noticing that his major poetry is commonly concerned with a character's difficult task of passing from one state of mind to another of which he (or she) has not previously been aware. Thus metaphors of bridging ("This Lime-Tree Bower My Prison"), transformation ("Frost at Midnight"), assimilation ("Christabel"), and awakening ("The Ancient Mariner") are frequent in his work.

28. By implication, at least, I have previously hazarded a guess at the reason. It may well be that the 1815 edition deliberately disguises the previously heterodox character of his religious thought,

and as Wordsworth aged his Anglican orthodoxy grew upon him.

29. Hazlitt, "On Shakespeare and Milton," *Complete Works,* 5:53.

30. Barbara Lewalski, "Innocence and Experience in Milton's Eden," *New Essays on Paradise Lost,* ed. Thomas Kranidas, p. 117.

31. Cf. J. A. Wittreich, Jr., *Angel of Apocalypse,* esp. "A Theory of Influence," pp. 223–29.

32. John Dennis, "The Grounds of Criticism in Poetry," *Critical Works,* 1:364, 366.

Bibliography

Primary Sources

Alison, Archibald. *Essays on the Nature and Principles of Taste.* 2 vols. Edinburgh, 1811.

Arnold, Matthew. *Essays in Criticism: Second Series.* London: Macmillan, 1905.

Avison, Charles. *Essays on Poetry and Music.* London, 1775.

Bacon, Francis. *Works.* Vol. I. London, 1826.

Blackwell, Thomas. *An Inquiry into the Life and Writings of Homer.* 2d ed. London, 1736.

Blair, Hugh. "A Critical Dissertation on the Poems of Ossian." *The Poems of Ossian.* Vol. 2. London, 1772.

———. *Lectures on Rhetoric and Belles Lettres.* Edited by Harold Harding. 2 vols. Carbondale: Southern Illinois University Press, 1965.

Blake, William. *The Poetry and Prose.* Edited by David Erdman and Harold Bloom. New York: Doubleday, 1965.

Boswell, James. *The Correspondence and Other Papers of James Boswell Relating to the Making of the Life of Johnson.* Edited by M. Waingrow. The Yale Editions of the Private Papers of James Boswell, edited by F. W. Hilles, vol. 2. New York: McGraw-Hill Book Co., 1969.

Burke, Edmund. *A Philosophical Enquiry into the Origins of Our Ideas of the Sublime and Beautiful.* Edited by J. T. Boulton. London: Routledge and Kegan Paul, 1958.

Chalmers, Alexander, ed. *The British Essayists.* Vol. 24. London, 1817.

Coleridge, Samuel Taylor. *Biographia Literaria.* Edited by J. Shawcross. 2 vols. London: Oxford University Press, 1958.

———. *The Poems.* Edited by Ernest Hartley Coleridge. 2 vols. Oxford: Clarendon Press, 1966.

Cooper, John Gilbert. *Letters Concerning Taste.* Edited by Ralph

Cohen. Augustan Reprint Society, Vol. 30. Los Angeles: University of California Press, 1951.

Dennis, John. *Critical Works*. Edited by E. N. Hooker. 2 vols. Baltimore: Johns Hopkins Press, 1939.

Dryden, John. *Essays*. Edited by W. P. Ker. 2 vols. New York: Russell and Russell, 1961.

Duff, William. *An Essay on Original Genius*. London, 1767.

Elledge, Scott, ed. *Eighteenth-Century Critical Essays*. 2 vols. Ithaca: Cornell University Press, 1961.

Gerard, Alexander. *An Essay on Genius*. London, 1774.

Gray, Thomas. *Correspondence*. Edited by Paget Toynbee and Leonard Whibley, with corrections and additions by H. W. Starr. 3 vols. Oxford: Clarendon Press, 1971.

Hartley, David. *Observations on Man*. 2 vols. London, 1791.

Hazlitt, William. *The Complete Works*. Edited by P. Howe. Vol. 5, London: J. M. Dent and Sons, 1930.

Hobbes, Thomas. *Leviathan*. Edited by A. R. Waller. Cambridge: Cambridge University Press, 1904.

Home, Henry, Lord Kames. *Elements of Criticism*. Edited by Abraham Mills. New York, 1847.

Hurd, Richard. *Letters on Chivalry and Romance*. Edited by Hoyt Trowbridge. Augustan Reprint Society, vols. 101-2. Los Angeles: University of California Press, 1963.

―――, ed. *Q. Horatii Flacci Epistolae ad Pisones et Augustum*. 3 vols. 4th ed. London: 1766.

Husbands, John, ed. *A Miscellany of Poems by Several Hands*. Oxford, 1731.

Johnson, Samuel. *Dictionary*. Edited by E. L. McAdam, Jr., and George Milne. New York: Pantheon Books, 1963.

―――. *Lives of the English Poets*. Edited by G. Birkbeck Hill. 3 vols. Oxford: Clarendon Press, 1905.

―――. Preface to Shakespeare. *Johnson on Shakespeare*. Edited by Arthur Sherbo, with introduction by Bertrand Bronson. The Yale Edition of the Works of Samuel Johnson, edited by E. C. McAdam, Jr., with Donald and Mary Hyde, vol. 7. New Haven: Yale University Press, 1968.

Jones, Sir William. *Poems*. Oxford, 1772.

Lonsdale, Roger, ed. *The Poems of Gray, Collins, and Goldsmith*. London: Longmans, 1969.

Lowth, Robert. *Lectures on the Sacred Poetry of the Hebrews*. 2 vols. London, 1787.

Pope, Alexander. *Literary Criticism*. Edited by Bernard Goldgar. Lincoln: University of Nebraska Press, 1965.

Reynolds, Frances. *An Inquiry Concerning the Principles of Taste, and the Origin of Our Ideas of Beauty*. Edited by James Clifford. Augustan Reprint Society, vol. 27. Los Angeles: University of California Press, 1951.

Rymer, Thomas. *The Critical Works*. Edited by Curt Zimansky. New Haven: Yale University Press, 1956.

Shenstone, William. *The Works in Verse and Prose*. 2 vols. London, 1764.

The Spectator. Edited by Donald F. Bond. 5 vols. Oxford: Clarendon Press, 1965.

Spingarn, J. E., ed. *Critical Essays of the Seventeenth Century*. 3 vols. London: Oxford University Press, 1957.

Trapp, Joseph. *Lectures on Poetry*. Hildesheim: Georg Olms Verlag, 1969.

Tucker, Abraham. *The Light of Nature Pursued*. 2 vols. London, 1852.

Warton, Joseph. *Collected Poetry*. The Collected Works of the English Poets, edited by A. Chalmers, vol. 18. London, 1810.

————. *Essay on the Genius and Writing of Pope*. Vol. 1, London, 1756; Vol. 2, London, 1782.

————, and John Warton, eds. *The Poetical Works of John Dryden*. London, 1867.

Warton, Thomas. *The History of English Poetry*. 4 vols. London, 1824.

————. *Observations on the Fairy Queen*. 2 vols. London, 1762.

————. *Poetical Works*. Edited by R. Mant. 2 vols. Oxford, 1802.

————, ed. *Poems upon Several Occasions . . . by John Milton*. London, 1791.

————, and Thomas Percy. *The Percy Letters: The Correspondence of Thomas Percy and Thomas Warton*. Edited by M. G. Robinson and Leah Dennis. Baton Rouge: Louisiana State University, 1951.

Webb, Daniel. *An Inquiry into the Beauties of Painting*. London, 1761.

————. *Remarks on the Beauties of Poetry*. London, 1762.

Wordsworth, William. *The Poetical Works*. Edited by E. De Selincourt. 5 vols. Oxford: Clarendon Press, 1940–1949.

————. *The Prose Works*. Edited by W. J. B. Owen and J. W. Smyser. 3 vols. Oxford: Clarendon Press, 1974.

————, and Dorothy Wordsworth. *The Letters of William and*

Dorothy Wordsworth: The Middle Years. Edited by E. De Selincourt. 2 vols. Oxford: Clarendon Press, 1937.

Secondary Sources

Abrams, M. H. *The Mirror and the Lamp*. New York: Oxford University Press, 1953.

————. *Natural Supernaturalism*. New York: W. W. Norton and Co., 1971.

Adams, Hazard. *William Blake: A Reading of the Shorter Poems*. Seattle: University of Washington Press, 1963.

Bate, W. J. *The Burden of the Past and the English Poet*. Cambridge: Harvard University Press, 1970.

————. *From Classic to Romantic*. Cambridge: Harvard University Press, 1946.

Beer, J. B. *Coleridge the Visionary*. London: Chatto and Windus, 1959.

Bloom, Harold. *Blake's Apocalypse: A Study in Poetic Argument*. New York: Doubleday, 1963.

Bottrall, Margaret, ed. *William Blake: Songs of Innocence and Experience: A Casebook*. London: Macmillan, 1970.

Brantley, Richard. *Wordsworth's "Natural Methodism."* New Haven: Yale University Press, 1975.

Bredvold, Louis. *The Natural History of Sensibility*. Detroit: Wayne State University Press, 1962.

Bronson, Bertrand. *Facets of the Enlightenment: Studies in English Literature and Its Contexts*. Berkeley: University of California Press, 1968.

————. "When Was Neoclassicism?" In *Studies in Criticism and Aesthetics, 1660–1800: Essays in Honor of Samuel Holt Monk*, edited by Howard Anderson and John Shea, pp. 13–25. Minneapolis: University of Minnesota Press, 1967.

Burke, Kenneth. *The Philosophy of Literary Form*. Baton Rouge: Louisiana State University Press, 1967.

Camden, Carroll, ed. *Restoration and Eighteenth-Century Literature*. Chicago: University of Chicago Press, 1963.

Cassirer, Ernst. *The Philosophy of the Enlightenment*. Princeton: Princeton University Press, 1951.

Chapin, Chester. *Personification in Eighteenth-Century English Poetry*. New York: King's Crown Press of Columbia University, 1955.

Chase, Stuart. *Quest for Myth*. Baton Rouge: Louisiana State University Press, 1949.

Cohen, Ralph. *The Art of Discrimination*. London: Routledge and Kegan Paul, 1964.

Crane, R. S., ed. *Critics and Criticism*. Chicago: University of Chicago Press, 1952.

Crider, J. R. "Structure and Effect in Collins's Progress Poems." *Studies in Philology* 60 (1963): 57–72.

Curtis, Jared. *Wordsworth's Experiments with Tradition*. Ithaca: Cornell University Press, 1971.

Doherty, F. "The Two Voices of Gray." *Essays in Criticism* 13 (1963): 222–30.

Downey, James, and Ben Jones, eds. *Fearful Joy*. Toronto: McGill-Queen's University Press, 1974.

Eliot, T. S. *Selected Essays*. New York: Harcourt Brace and Co., 1932.

Empson, William. *Seven Types of Ambiguity*. Norfolk, Conn.: New Directions, 1949.

Ende, Stuart A. *Keats and the Sublime*. New Haven: Yale University Press, 1976.

Erdman, David, and John Grant, eds. *Blake's Visionary Forms Dramatic*. Princeton: Princeton University Press, 1970.

Ferry, David. *The Limits of Mortality*. Middletown, Conn.: Wesleyan University Press, 1959.

Fletcher, Angus. *Allegory: The Theory of a Symbolic Mode*. Ithaca: Cornell University Press, 1964.

Frye, Northrop. *Fearful Symmetry*. Princeton: Princeton University Press, 1947.

―――. "Towards Defining an Age of Sensibility." *ELH* 23 (1956): 144–52.

―――, ed. *Blake: A Collection of Critical Essays*. New York: Prentice-Hall, 1966.

Fussell, Paul. *The Rhetorical World of Augustan Humanism*. London: Oxford University Press, 1965.

Gleckner, Robert. *The Piper and the Bard*. Detroit: Wayne State University Press, 1959.

Hagstrum, Jean. *Samuel Johnson's Literary Criticism*. Chicago: University of Chicago Press, 1967.

―――. *The Sister Arts*. Chicago: University of Chicago Press, 1958.

_____. *William Blake: Poet and Painter.* Chicago: University of Chicago Press, 1964.

Hartman, Geoffrey. *Wordsworth's Poetry, 1787–1814.* New Haven: Yale University Press, 1964.

Hayden, John. *The Romantic Reviewers, 1802–1824.* London: Routledge and Kegan Paul, 1969.

Helmstadter, T. H. "Blake's *Night Thoughts:* Interpretations of Edward Young." *Texas Studies in Literature and Language* 12 (1970): 27–54.

Hilles, F. W., and Harold Bloom, eds. *From Sensibility to Romanticism.* New York: Oxford University Press, 1965.

Hipple, W. J. *The Beautiful, the Sublime, and the Picturesque in Eighteenth-Century British Aesthetic Theory.* Carbondale: Southern Illinois University Press, 1957.

Hirsch, E. D. *Innocence and Experience: An Introduction to Blake.* New Haven: Yale University Press, 1964.

Jack, Ian. *Augustan Satire.* Oxford: Clarendon Press, 1952.

Johnston, Arthur. *Enchanted Ground.* London: University of London Press, 1964.

Jordan, Frank, ed. *The English Romantic Poets: A Review of Research and Criticism.* New York: Modern Language Association of America, 1972.

Kranidas, Thomas, ed. *New Essays on Paradise Lost.* Berkeley: University of California Press, 1969.

Manwaring, Elizabeth. *Italian Landscape in Eighteenth Century England.* New York: Oxford University Press, 1925.

Miles, Josephine. *Eras and Modes in English Poetry.* Berkeley: University of California Press, 1957.

Miner, Earl. "Mr. Dryden and Mr. Rymer." *Philological Quarterly* 54 (1975): 137–51.

Monk, Samuel Holt. *The Sublime: A Study of Critical Theories in Eighteenth-Century England.* New York: Modern Language Association of America, 1935.

Morris, David B. *The Religious Sublime: Christian Poetry and Critical Tradition in Eighteenth-Century England.* Lexington: University of Kentucky Press, 1972.

Nicolson, Marjorie Hope. *Mountain Gloom and Mountain Glory: The Development of the Aesthetics of the Infinite.* Ithaca: Cornell University Press, 1959.

Owen, W. J. B. *Wordsworth as Critic.* Toronto: University of Toronto Press, 1969.

Pittock, Joan. *The Ascendancy of Taste: The Achievement of Joseph and Thomas Warton.* London: Routledge and Kegan Paul. 1973.

Potts, Abbie Findlay. *Wordsworth's "Prelude": A Study of Its Literary Form.* Ithaca: Cornell University Press, 1953.

Poulet, Georges. *The Metamorphoses of the Circle.* Baltimore: Johns Hopkins University Press, 1966.

Praz, Mario. *The Romantic Agony.* London: Oxford University Press, 1933.

Prickett, Stephen. *Coleridge and Wordsworth: The Poetry of Growth.* Cambridge: Cambridge University Press, 1970.

Raine, Kathleen. *Blake and Tradition.* 2 vols. Princeton: Princeton University Press, 1968.

Reed, Mark. *Wordsworth: The Chronology of the Middle Years, 1800–1815.* Cambridge: Harvard University Press, 1975.

Sigworth, Oliver. *William Collins.* New York: Twayne Press, 1965.

Spacks, P. M. "Artful Strife: Conflict in Gray's Poetry." *PMLA* 81 (1966): 63–69.

———. *The Insistence of Horror.* Cambridge: Harvard University Press, 1962.

———. *The Poetry of Vision.* Cambridge: Harvard University Press, 1967.

Tayler, Irene, ed. *Blake's Illustrations to the Poems of Gray.* Princeton: Princeton University Press, 1971.

Thorpe, Clarence. *The Aesthetic Theory of Thomas Hobbes.* Ann Arbor: University of Michigan Press, 1940.

Tuve, Rosemond. *Images and Themes in Five Poems by Milton.* Cambridge: Harvard University Press, 1957.

Tuveson, Ernest. *The Imagination as a Means of Grace.* Berkeley: University of California Press, 1960.

Wain, John, ed. *Contemporary Reviews of Romantic Poetry.* New York: Barnes and Noble, 1953.

Wasserman, Earl. "The Inherent Values of Eighteenth-Century Personification." *PMLA* 65 (1950): 435–63.

Watt, Ian. "The Comic Syntax of *Tristram Shandy.*" In *Studies in Criticism and Aesthetics, 1660–1800: Essays in Honor of Samuel Holt Monk,* edited by Howard Anderson and John Shea, pp.

315–31. Minneapolis: University of Minnesota Press, 1967.

Weiskel, Thomas. *The Romantic Sublime*. Baltimore: Johns Hopkins University Press, 1976.

Wittreich, J. A., Jr. *Angel of Apocalypse: Blake's Idea of Milton*. Madison: University of Wisconsin Press, 1975.

Wlecke, Albert. *Wordsworth and the Sublime*. Berkeley: University of California Press, 1973.

Index